Continuous Improvement
in the
Science Classroom

Also Available from ASQ Quality Press

Improving Student Learning: Applying Deming's Quality Principles in Classrooms
Lee Jenkins

Thinking Tools for Kids: An Activity Book for Classroom Learning
Barbara A. Cleary, Ph.D. and Sally J. Duncan

Futuring Tools for Strategic Quality Planning in Education
William F. Alexander and Richard W. Serfass

Quality Team Learning for Schools: A Principal's Perspective
James E. Abbott

The New Philosophy for K–12 Education: A Deming Framework for Transforming America's Schools
James F. Leonard

Creating Dynamic Teaching Teams in Schools
K. Mark Kevesdy and Tracy A. Burich, with contributions from Kelly A. Spier

Success Through Quality: Support Guide for the Journey to Continuous Improvement
Timothy J. Clark

Puzzling Quality Puzzles
J.P. Russell and Janice Russell

To request a complimentary catalog of ASQ Quality Press publication, call 800-248-1946.

Continuous Improvement in the Science Classroom

Jeffrey J. Burgard

ASQ Quality Press
Milwaukee, Wisconsin

Continuous Improvement in the Science Classroom
Jeffrey J. Burgard

Library of Congress Cataloging-in-Publication Data

Burgard, Jeffrey J., 1964–
    Continuous improvement in the science classroom / by Jeffrey J. Burgard.
       p.   cm.
    Includes bibliographical references (p.   ) and index.
    ISBN 0-87389-434-0 (alk. paper)
    1. Science—Study and teaching (Middle school)   2. Science—Study and
teaching (Secondary)   I. Title.
    Q181.B93   1999
    507'.1'273—dc21
                          99-38548
                          CIP

10 9 8 7 6 5 4 3 2 1

ISBN 0-87389-434-0

Acquisitions Editor: Ken Zielske

Project Editor: Annemieke Koudstaal

Production Administrator: Shawn Dohogne

ASQ Mission: The American Society for Quality advances individual and organizational performance excellence worldwide by providing opportunities for learning, quality improvement, and knowledge exchange.

Attention: Bookstores, Wholesalers, Schools and Corporations:
ASQ Quality Press books, videotapes, audiotapes, and software are available at quantity discounts with bulk purchases for business, educational, or instructional use. For information, please contact ASQ Quality Press at 800-248-1946, or write to ASQ Quality Press, P.O. Box 3005, Milwaukee, WI 53201-3005.

To place orders or to request a free copy of the ASQ Quality Press Publications Catalog, including ASQ membership information, call 800-248-1946. Visit our web site at http://www.asq.org.

Printed in the United States of America

∞ Printed on acid-free paper

American Society for Quality

ASQ

Quality Press
611 East Wisconsin Avenue
Milwaukee, Wisconsin 53202
Call toll free 800-248-1946
http://www.asq.org
http://standardsgroup.asq.org

Dedication

This book is dedicated to the many people who helped write it: My parents, Joe and Fran Burgard, who give unlimited and unconditional love and support to all that I do; my grandmother, Maxine Hjelte, for the expert proofreading that only she could give, and last but not least, to the students past and present of Team USA, Camelot, and all others that I have had the privilege to have in my classroom. Without them, and their wonderful feedback and ideas, this book would never have been possible. I'm honored to have shared in a part of their lives. Thanks for being my inspiration, my challenge, and my guinea pigs.

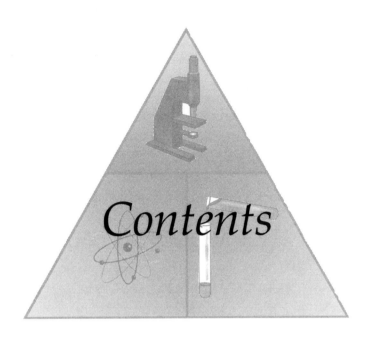

Contents

SECTION 1 THE SYSTEMS THINKING SCIENCE CLASSROOM

*Improving the science teacher's awareness of the
system in and around the classroom.*

SECTION 2 EPISTEMOLOGY

Improving student learning.

SECTION 3 PSYCHOLOGY

Improving student enthusiasm, behavior, and performance.

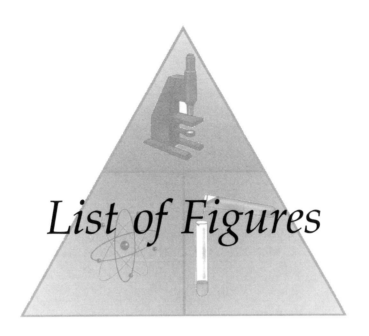

List of Figures

Chapter 2

Chapter 5

Chapter 6

Chapter 8

Chapter 9

Chapter 10

Foreword
by Lee Jenkins

The books in the ASQ Continuous Series are written for teachers who possess both the utmost respect for their students and a desire to improve student learning. Teachers are often frustrated because the tools society provides for student improvement do not honor their respect for students.

Four currently popular methods for improving student learning are these: (1) add more fear to the lives of students; (2) bribe students with incentives to do better or more work; (3) set up false competition between students; and (4) purchase a new program and demand its use.

There are, however, thousands of teachers who love and respect their students and recognize that fear, bribery, false competition, and my-way-or-the-highway approaches don't work. At best they achieve short-term results. The books in the ASQ Continuous Improvement Series, by Fauss, Burgard, Carson, and Ayres Mercer, are written from the hearts of teachers who possess the two criteria mentioned in the first paragraph. They love and respect their students while maintaining an intense desire to improve their students' learning.

These teachers clearly describe their experiences with a fifth option: studying and using data for continual improvements. They document the systems their classrooms use to collect weekly data, as well as the process of making curricular decisions based upon their data. The data is from students' long-term memories. There is no place for cramming and short-term memory. The teachers and their students, functioning as a team, can and do plan their improvements. They know within a few weeks if the instructional plans are working or not. No longer must these teachers wait until July to see results.

Readers will enjoy these teachers' experiences and stories, but most of all they will learn exactly how to restructure the management of their classroom learning systems toward significant improvement.

Each of the four authors in the ASQ Continuous Improvement Series brings a unique view of quality processes into his or her classroom.

Fauss: In the culture of education, teachers call themselves lucky when they have an exceptionally bright class. The unstated inference is that the next year will return to normal. What happens, however, when a teacher is determined to prove that every year will end with better results than the previous year? After a year or two, this becomes intense, because the easy ideas are used up. Even though her examples come from language arts, the structure Fauss describes for continuous improvement can be used in any subject.

Burgard: It is clear that Burgard sees the application of quality principles through the eyes of a scientist. He changed the English department's rubric into a dichotomous key, and he analyzed student writing errors like a chemist. Further, he knows science is not science unless it can be replicated. This means students must have precise knowledge of definitions and clear understanding of scientific processes. Both information and knowledge are essential; there's no room for an educational pendulum in Burgard's thinking.

Carson: Most surveys of school attitude document that history/social science is the most hated of school subjects. Readers of Carson's book will easily see, however, why history is her students' favorite subject. Not only are they loving to learn the facts of history, they are thinking like historians. She pushes student involvement in planning further than I've ever seen—even including scheduling lessons and assignments. This is not just the Carson show—it's better.

Ayres Mercer: This book combines the principles of quality with research taken from the Third International Math and Science Study (TIMSS). As a part of this study, videos were made that demonstrate Japanese methods of teaching mathematics. Ayres Mercer has combined these Japanese methods with principles of quality. Her work is truly unique in the world of mathematics education. Further, she documents her students' growth in mathematics concepts weekly, and their attitude toward mathematics monthly. Her formula for success is this:

*mathematics concepts + mathematics problem solving + great attitudes +
the data to prove each is occurring = great school mathematics*

The poorer an idea, the more age specific it is; the better the idea, the wider the age span it has. Even though these four teachers each teach a particular grade and relate stories about a particular age group, audiences from kindergarten through college may benefit from their provocative lessons.

Preface

I have been continually frustrated, throughout my career, about how to effectively improve my classroom environment, evaluate my students, and know that the "improvements" made have been successful. I could say that I felt improvement had happened, but I had no way of showing it. No conference or workshop gave me lessons or ideas that helped me. I was doing a good job, but I could never show it concretely.

The key was in how I was approaching the classroom. I felt as if I were in an isolated box. There were so many things outside the class that I couldn't control, that I held tightly to the control I felt I had there. The students seemed to be just a group of boys and girls that came into my room at the beginning of the year and left at the end, coming from nowhere and headed for somewhere.

The *Systems Thinking* and *Continuous Improvement* philosophies that I am proposing in this book require that the science teacher see outside the classroom into the bigger picture of the child's education. It's an outlook that makes the science classroom a part of the whole system, rather than isolating it from the rest of the school system. Approaching the science classroom as part of a system, rather than as an independent island, requires teachers to be more focused on what students need to know when they enter their classrooms, as well as when they leave.

This way of thinking has helped me cement the facts that the students need to know into their long-term memories without doing rote memorization. This allows more time to guide, instruct, and evaluate true knowledge and application. It has made me a coach in the classroom. It *is* possible to get the students to remember the *facts* and have a *hands-on* science classroom! Many people may think this is impossible, which is much like the attitude prevalent in the United States in the fifties and sixties toward producing high quality/low price products: It was thought you could only have one or the other.

Not only does this book help science teachers manage student learning, but it also gives teachers a way to gain feedback to make students a vital part of the system. When we use Deming's reasoning that 96 percent of problems are system problems, the habit of blaming the students for problems disappears, and ways to improve the system emerge. By using student feedback, both positive and negative, during the school year, the teacher can get the information needed to improve the classroom system and meet the students' needs. That feedback can carry over year to year so that the classroom evolves. Future students and the teacher are benefactors of suggestions made by the former students. Furthermore, parent feedback can also be acquired so that the parents can become an active part of the improving classroom system.

Continuous Improvement in the Science Classroom also provides the critical components needed to balance the new accountability of the statewide standardized tests with the integrity of real science-based programs. It shows a way for teachers to improve student test scores without just "teaching to the test."

This book is intended to show the science teacher how to apply the principles of *profound knowledge* to make science classrooms a more effective learning environment. *This book is not theory.* This is not a new idea or boxed program. There is no step-by-step guide or specific lesson plan included. It is, by its nature, a philosophy. It is a practical guide to the way that I have adapted and applied quality principals in an eighth grade science classroom. It describes practical science classroom applications for the tools and techniques used in the business world when implementing total quality management (TQM). It is a new application of proven theories and techniques. This book is filled with ideas on how to apply improvement processes that I hope will spur you on to greater ideas. These tools provide a way to gain statistical data to prove to the teacher, the administration, the state, the parents, and the students that learning is occurring.

The application of this philosophy doesn't require a complete change of program as much as it requires a shift in thinking. These changes in thinking translate into only a few adjustments in the classroom. *They will not cost more money or require countless hours of time!* To apply this philosophy will take only a few hours of preparation, and less than ten dollars for an *optional* one-time purchase of a hundred-sided die. These dice can be purchased at a local school-supply store, game shop, or from the manufacturer: Games Science, 7604 Newton Drive R9, North Biloxi, MS. 39532. There is also the *optional* purchase of the software program *Class Action*™, available through the publisher of this book, ASQ Quality Press. It can be ordered at 1-800-248-1946, item number SW1064. This software makes keeping track of the data much easier, but it is optional.

I welcome you to the ideas of *Continuous Improvement in the Science Classroom* and I hope that you see as many benefits in this program as I have. If nothing else, I hope that these ideas serve as a way to make improvement the focus in your class. Or I hope they serve as a launch pad for your own ideas, which may be much better than mine. This book itself is under continuous improvement . In the 18 months it took to write it, many new ideas and improvements needed to be added. The nice thing about improving is that there is no end to it. I wish you joy and adventure in your quest to improve your science classroom!

JEFF BURGARD
REDDING, CALIFORNIA, 1999

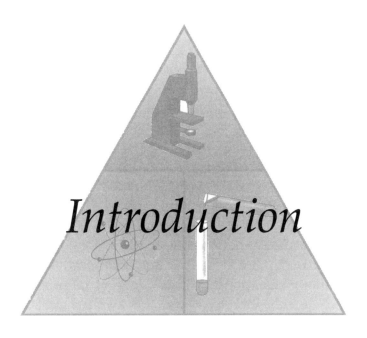

Introduction

This book is loosely based on the work of Dr. W. Edwards Deming and his theories of profound knowledge and continuous improvement. The approach used is an extension, or an application, of the theories written and proposed by Dr. Lee Jenkins in his book *Improving Student Learning*. It is one in a four-book series that gives practical classroom applications to Dr. Jenkins's theories. Each book is specific to a subject area: Math, science, history, and reading and writing in the primary classroom. Although the theory in each book is the same, the individual subject matter applications are a little different. This book is the application in the science classroom. Before proceeding, it is important that a little background is given so that it is understood who Dr. Deming was and what he did.

Dr. W. Edwards Deming is one of the most influential, but least known, individuals of our time. He was an expert in the field of statistical process control. This is a method for consistently improving the quality of goods and services using data. Deming's teachings and philosophies on management, when applied to business, created the "Japanese Industrial Miracle" in the early 1950s. Japan became the world's industrial leader seemingly overnight. Japanese companies were able to produce a high-quality product at a low price. At the time, this was thought to be impossible. The prevailing thought was that high quality would be high priced and low quality low priced. This "miracle" was accomplished by using Deming's concepts to form what is now known as total quality management. This management system is centered in his famous *14 Points of Management*. He believed *people* are the driving force for improvement in a system, and that management is to be held responsible for any failure that occurs within the system. He proposed that 96 percent of the problems faced by employers are those of the system, not of the personnel. Employees work within the system. Employers and management, however, are responsible for working *on* the system. By using employee input, the management can change the system to make it better for the workers, as well as to create better products and reduce defects. It was this belief, and the practices that it inspired, that built the employee morale that played a large part in increasing the quality of products made at the Japanese factories.

Although used by the United States before and during World War II to create high-quality weapons and armaments, Deming and his quality philosophy were quickly forgotten after the war. America's industrial machine geared up for the high postwar demand, and *quality* was sacrificed for *quantity*. Deming wasn't rediscovered by U.S. manufacturers until they went to Japan in the late 1970s to find out how the Japanese produced high-quality, low-priced products. He then had a great influence in America from 1980 until his death in 1993.

The first inroads of Deming's philosophy into education were made in the administrative aspects of the school system. The job of school administration is managing, so this is where Dr. Deming's management philosophies could be most easily incorporated. I have had the privilege of working in the Enterprise School District in Redding, California, since 1991 under the leadership of Dr. Lee Jenkins. Dr. Jenkins is the author of *Improving Student Learning* and an authority in the operation of a school district based on Deming Philosophy. I have also read numerous books and attended conferences and seminars by experts in quality philosophy and how it theoretically could be applied to classrooms.

Through these avenues, I saw how I could incorporate the philosophy into my classroom. The science classroom is also a place of management. Teachers not only have to manage people, but also have to manage learning. This is where Deming's theory of profound knowledge comes in.

Profound knowledge simply says that learning cannot be based on experiences only, but requires comparisons of results to a prediction, plan, or theory. It sounds a lot like the scientific method to me. According to Deming's book *The New Economics*, profound knowledge contains four interrelated parts. They are:

1. Appreciation for a System

2. Theory of Knowledge

3. Psychology

4. Knowledge about Variation

Each part of profound knowledge and its application to the science classroom is described in this book. The first three each have an entire section devoted to them: Section 1 is devoted to the system. Section 2 is devoted to epistemology, or the theory of knowledge. Section 3 deals with psychology. Variation is covered throughout the book, but especially in Section 4.

The scientific method has always been applied to experiments in the science classroom, but rarely to the classroom itself. This book then is not about how to teach science, but how to approach the classroom with a plan for continuously improving all aspects of profound knowledge.

THE SYSTEMS THINKING SCIENCE CLASSROOM

"A ship can do no better than its design will allow."

W. EDWARDS DEMING

Improving the science teacher's awareness of the system in and around the classroom.

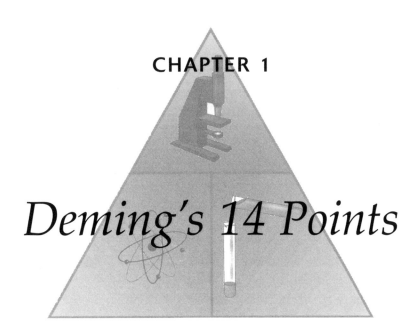

CHAPTER 1

Deming's 14 Points

Ⅰn setting down the guidelines for the quality philosophy of management, W. Edwards Deming devised *14 points* that have since become the "Ten Commandments" of total quality throughout the world. These are used in business as a way of managing people to make a product or conduct a service. Teachers can use these 14 points because they manage people and learning.

Since these *14 points* aren't always worded in a way that makes sense in a science classroom setting, I have taken the liberty here of rewording them to make them more applicable. I will refer to these principles where they apply throughout the book. Here are the *14 points* as they are worded for business, from Dr. Deming's book *Out of the Crisis*, and my translation to make them apply to the science classroom. Some are out of order because they cover similar topics and are grouped together.

Deming's First Point

Create consistency of purpose toward improvement of product and service, with the aim of becoming competitive, staying in business, and providing jobs.

My Adaptation: Create consistency of purpose toward improvement of the students and the teaching, with the aim of producing knowledgeable students who can compete in the global marketplace.

Deming's Second Point

Adopt the new philosophy. We are in a new economic age. Western management must awaken to the challenge, learn their responsibilities, and take on leadership for a change.

My Adaptation: Adopt the new philosophy. We are in a new educational age. Public schools must awaken to the challenge, define their purpose, and set an example.

Deming's Third Point

Cease dependence on inspection to achieve quality. Eliminate the need for inspection on a mass basis by building quality into the product in the first place.

My Adaptation: Cease dependence on testing to achieve quality. Eliminate the need for mass standardized testing by building quality into the students in the first place.

Deming's Fourth Point

End the practice of rewarding business on the basis of price tag. Instead minimize total cost. Move toward a single supplier for any one item, on a long-term relationship of loyalty and trust.

My Adaptation: Upper-grade teachers must work with lower-grade teachers to gain understanding of what will be expected in their classes. The aim is not only to give the students the skills to survive the current year, but minimize failure and create lifelong learners.

Deming's Fifth Point

Improve constantly and forever the system of production and service, in order to improve quality and productivity and thus constantly decrease cost.

My Adaptation: Constantly improve every activity in the classroom, in order to improve the quality and production of the teacher and each student, while decreasing the likelihood of failure.

Deming's Sixth and Thirteenth Points

Sixth—Institute training on the job.

Thirteenth—Institute a vigorous program of education and self-improvement.

My Adaptation: Train teachers and students in the continuous improvement process, and in understanding the implications of viewing their classrooms as true systems.

Deming's Seventh, Tenth, and Eleventh Points

Seventh—Institute leadership. The aim of supervision should be to help people and machines and gadgets to do a better job. Supervision of management is in need of overhaul, as is supervision of production workers.

Tenth—Eliminate slogans, exhortations, and targets that call for the work force to have zero defects and new levels of productivity. Such exhortations only create adversarial relationships, as the bulk of the causes of low quality and productivity belong to the system, and thus lie beyond the power of the work force.

Eleventh—a) Eliminate work standards that prescribe numerical quotas for the day. Substitute leadership. b) Eliminate management by objective. Eliminate management by numbers, numerical goals. Substitute leadership.

 My Adaptation: The purpose of the teacher is to help the students improve in all that they do and achieve all that they can achieve. This is done by removing the barriers within the classroom system that hinder enthusiasm and learning.

Deming's Eighth Point

Drive out fear, so that everyone may work effectively for the company.

 My Adaptation: Do not manage the classroom through threats and fear. Work with the students so that they may work most effectively.

Deming's Ninth Point

Break down the barriers between departments. People in research, design, sales, and production must work as a team to foresee problems in production and in use that may be encountered with the product or the service.

 My Adaptation: Break down the barriers between departments. Teachers, grade levels, administrators, schools, disciplines, parents, and students all need to work together to foresee problems and create an effective learning community.

Deming's Twelfth Point

First, remove barriers that rob the hourly worker of pride in workmanship. The responsibility of supervisors must be changed from sheer numbers to quality.

Second, remove the barriers that rob people in management and in engineering of their right to pride in workmanship. This means, *inter alia*, abolition of the annual or merit rating and of management by objective.

 My Adaptation: Students must be put in charge of their own continuous improvement and be motivated intrinsically so that they take pride in their accomplishments. Take away grading based on number of assignments turned in, and give the students criteria for high quality and help them to achieve it.

Deming's Fourteenth Point

Put everyone in the company in teams to accomplish the transformation. The transformation is everybody's job.

 My Adaptation: Collect and take in feedback from parents, administrators, and students to make them part of the process of designing the best science program imaginable.

All of Deming's *14 points* are easily translatable into the classroom setting. The management that a classroom teacher has to do on a daily basis is equal to some of the toughest managerial jobs in industry. Teachers can use the tools that industry has begun to use, in order to more effectively manage their classrooms and make the most of themselves and of their students.

Key Points

- All of Deming's 14 points of management are easily transferred to the science classroom.

- They are transferable from business because in the science classroom, teachers are managing *people* and *learning*.

- A teacher's job of managing a room of 30 people at different ability levels, to accomplish a common goal, is equal to some of the most challenging business management roles.

- Teachers, therefore, need to learn and use the same tools of management that businesses use to handle such challenges.

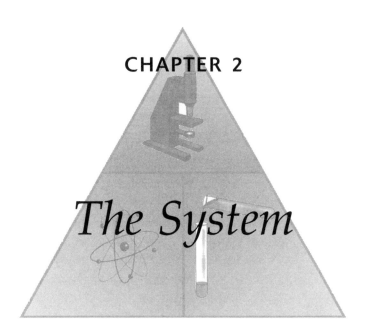

CHAPTER 2

The System

Part 1
Seeing the System in the Classroom

In order to make improvements in the classroom, teachers must view the classroom differently. Teachers teach in a school *system*. All schools, classrooms, students, teachers, and parents are linked together in a delicate web that forms the fabric of a child's education. Nothing within the system exists in isolation. Very few people, however, take the time or make the effort to think about how this system is composed. There is a movement, especially in recent years, to view the schools and districts with systems thinking, yet *the classroom is a system too*. A science teacher needs to look at the system that exists in and around his classroom to understand how it operates and how it can be improved.

One of the core philosophies in the Deming approach is that when problems exist, they are very rarely people problems. He believed that 95 to 97 percent of problems are system problems and the other 3 to 5 percent are people problems. In other words, a problem most likely exists in the way that people are treated, in the way the operation is organized, or in the inability of the parts of the system to communicate, rather than with personnel.

In a classroom, teachers often blame the students when things are not going well. Many teachers say that students are irresponsible, lazy, or not as smart and respectful as they used to be. Students will say that teachers are boring or uncaring. Blaming people never helps, and it certainly doesn't solve problems. Systems thinking takes the blame out and puts a problem-solving approach to work, so that together problems are solved. Before applying systems thinking, however, teachers need to understand the parts of a system and how they apply to the classroom.

Figure 2.1 is a picture of the system that exists in a school district. Figure 2.2 depicts the system in a classroom. Compare the two. As stated before, nothing within the system exists in isolation. All parts affect all other parts. This is an essential understanding that has to be acknowledged before attempting any solution. How solutions will affect the other parts of the system has to be considered constantly. Here is a brief look at each of these parts and how it applies to the science classroom.

Aim

Each classroom needs to have some setting that it is trying to obtain or achieve. The aim of the classroom needs to be clearly defined and easy to understand. This is the classroom's focus. The students should know what they and the teacher are trying to accomplish.

Supply

For each individual classroom, the supply consists of all the students in lower grades before they enter his/her classroom. They are the raw material that the teacher molds and then sends on to the customers. Students come from somewhere. Is there a way that the teacher can actually help to prepare his own supply?

Input

Input in the classroom includes budgets, laws, court rulings, class size, facilities, text, materials, furniture, and so on. It is an area that very few teachers actually have in their control, so it will not be discussed in this book.

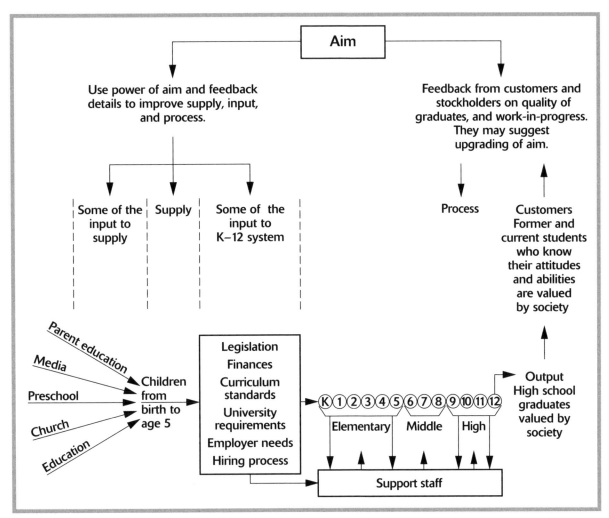

Figure 2.1. A school district system.

Process

The process in the classroom is the way in which teachers present their curriculums. There are many methods and styles that are used around the world. This is where individuals shine and the methods used are very personal. This book is not intended to convince a teacher to change the way she teaches. However, it will provide a different way of looking at teaching, and a way to gather statistical data to inform and improve instruction.

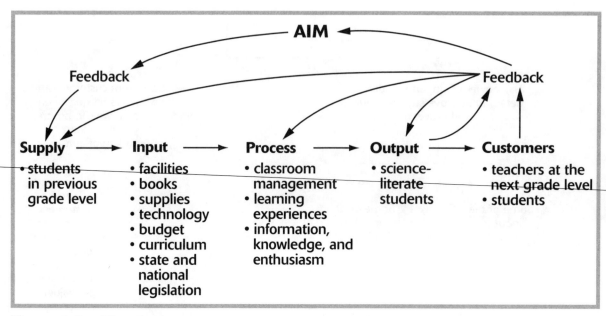

Figure 2.2. The classroom as a system.

Output

What does a classroom produce? At the end of the school year, another group of students has passed through the school system, and their learning has become the product of that system. Teachers need to have a goal of sending out better and better product each year. This can be accomplished by gathering clear statistical data, and using that data to improve instruction. This makes it possible to see if students are getting better. This book helps teachers to use data to monitor whether or not they are meeting the "continuous improvement" goal.

Customers

Schools have many customers with a wide range of demands. There are both internal and external customers. These include the following:

External customers

Society—wants functional and literate citizens.

Business—wants better, more qualified employees with applicable skills and the ability to solve problems.

Next year's teachers—want incoming students to know the prerequisite work that supports their curriculums, and to have acceptable behavior.

Parents—all want different things. Some parents want their children to have good grades, regardless of understanding. Other parents want their children to gain skills and knowledge. Others are happy if school is nothing more than a safe place for six hours a day.

Internal customers

The students—are the most immediate and the most important customers. Teachers need to gain feedback from students to help inform and improve their instruction, and to create an environment where students feel a sense of belonging, ownership, and purpose.

Feedback

In order for a system to improve, there has to be feedback. Feedback can be positive or negative, but improvement comes only with the knowledge of what to improve. Teachers need to gain feedback from a variety of sources. They need to know how the students are feeling, and what they are learning. Teachers need to know how they met the needs of their previous students and if they are meeting the needs of their current parents. Luckily, there are tools for gathering and assessing such feedback.

The classroom is a living, breathing, and dynamic system. By understanding the big picture of what parts are involved in the classroom, teachers can look for ways to improve each part so that the entire system may function better.

Part 2
Systems Thinking: Into and Beyond the Science Classroom

Deming's Ninth Point (adapted for the science classroom)

Break down the barriers between departments. Teachers, grade levels, administrators, schools, disciplines, parents, and students all need to work together to create an effective learning community.

Looking at the classroom in a systems model made much more sense to me when I heard it compared to big business. I heard a true story that I will now retell about a car company and the reason it needed to shift to systems thinking.

Before W. Edwards Deming's philosophies came to the United States, manufacturers viewed their world—much as many classroom teachers view their classes today—as an isolated entity. Contracts to suppliers went to the cheapest bidder, not to the producer of the highest quality. The contracts were short term, and there was no commitment past the term of the contract. This story deals with one such manufacturer, a car company, and its effort to obtain tires for its cars. This car company, like most others, bought its tires on these short-term, lowest-price contracts for years. When a shipment of tires came in from a tire company, the car company's inspector returned any tires that didn't meet the company's standard. What he didn't know was that the tire company would simply rewrap the rejected tires and send them back on the next shipment. If the tires didn't pass again, the tire manufacturer would find out when the rejecting inspector had his day off, and send the tires again. The tires that failed originally would often pass eventually. If the tires were continually rejected, the tire company would simply rewrap the same rejected tires and try another car company. With no long-term commitment between customer and supplier, there was no reason to invest the capital needed to make better tires. The result was a decline in the overall quality of the car and a dissatisfaction among the buying public.

Deming suggested that the problem could be fixed with systems thinking. If the car manufacturers viewed the supplier as part of its system, instead of as a separate unrelated entity, it would make a big difference. The car company decided to negotiate with one tire company and set up a long-term contract. A long-term arrangement meant that the tire company could count on orders, and would feel comfortable making investments to improve the quality. With better tires, the car company could produce a better overall product for its customer. The tire company, the car manufacturer, and the car buyer would all benefit.

How does this apply to the classroom? A teacher can look at his classroom in the very same way! The teacher can ask, "Who is *my supplier* and who are *my customers*?"

Suppliers and Customers

If the "supply" is the students coming into the class, then the suppliers must be the previous teacher and the parents. It also follows that one of the customers is the next year's teacher.

When I first came to my middle school, I experienced something similar to the car and tire companies' relationship. There were negative feelings toward both the elementary teachers and the high school teachers. When students with few skills came to us from elementary grades, we blamed their teachers. The high school, in turn, blamed us when the students we sent to them didn't seem prepared for their classes. Now society blames the schools for uneducated masses. Blame is not a problem-solving tool. The similarities between communication and methods in schools now, and those in business before systems thinking, are staggering. The following is a recent example from my district. See if you can see the similarities.

At the eighth-grade level, the math department was told that the high school math department needed assessments for proper placement in its high school math program. All eighth-grade students were given a test. In addition, the teachers were asked to recommend student placement in the different high school classes. The eighth-grade teachers were given a choice between a variety of classes, but no descriptions accompanied those classes. They were making recommendations based upon what they thought the classes were like. No one knew the difference between Math A and Basic Math. They just made recommendations and figured that the assessments would do the final sorting.

When dialogue between the math departments finally began, the junior high math department found out that not only had the math department at the high school never seen any test results, they had never even asked for the tests to be given in the first place. Somehow the counseling department at the high school was conducting these tests and not sharing the results. The high school teachers received students in their classes at the beginning of the year, based only on the eighth-grade teachers' uninformed recommendations. Then midway through the first quarter, the high school teachers had to do a mad shuffle to get the students into the proper classes. They were upset with the way we had recommended the students and they silently blamed us for their troubles.

The supplier of educated young adults in America is the school system, yet the communication between schools and grade levels is amazingly sparse and inconsistent. Even on a small scale, such as the example of the math departments, communication is just now starting to happen. There is even a lack of communication between classrooms and grade levels at the same school!

The parallel between this school situation and that of the car and tire companies is real. Just as the corporations began to look at their world as a *system*, it is time for schools and classrooms to do the same.

This process of coordination between schools or grade levels is, in essence, developing a relationship between customer and supplier. It wasn't an overnight process for the auto industry, and it won't be for the schools. It will be a process of continuous improvement toward that goal. The important part is the willingness to view things from this perspective. It is a *system* problem, not a problem with teachers' individual programs. Nearly all of the teachers I know are working long hours to provide the best education possible for their students. It is not the teachers who need to be fixed, but rather the system that needs to be adjusted. Together, with patience and determination, it can be done.

Improving Relations with the Supply

It is easy to see the students as our supply in this example. Manufacturers, however, don't need to know or to have a relationship with their supplies. Teachers, on the other hand, are dealing with human beings, not cold pieces of metal. The students have free will and feelings. They need a sense of belonging and value, and they need to feel a connection with their surroundings. Yet every year the students are put into unfamiliar classrooms with teachers they don't know. If this was just a problem for the students it would be one thing, but the teachers are also suddenly faced with between 30 and 180 students whom they don't know, and are expected to teach them. The first few days or weeks of school are usually spent getting to know each other and forming expectations. There needs to be a way for teachers and students to be more familiar with each other before the first day of school.

As a favor to a colleague who taught seventh grade science, I substituted in his class for a period. When the students first walked into the classroom that day, they thought they had a normal substitute. I recognized the "this-is-going-to-be-fun" smirk appearing on some of their faces when they realized their regular teacher was not there. What really shocked me was that even though I taught two doors down the hall, none of them knew who I was, and I didn't know them.

The first thing I said to them was, "I'm not a normal sub. I teach eighth grade two doors down the hall and I have some expectations for your behavior. Listen closely because many of you may be in my class next year!" Instantly the feeling in the room changed. A teacher from a higher grade level is scary to those in a lower grade level. The students sat up, closed their mouths and listened. I told them exactly what I expected of them, and that it was the same as I expected from my eighth graders. They now had their first glimpse of what they could expect from me and they knew that they would see me again. I had begun a relationship with my supply, and I used the opportunity to plant seeds of expectation in their minds.

That one period helped me to understand how I could work with my supply. There were many unexpected benefits. It was wonderful when the students that were in that seventh grade class would now say "hi" in the halls and even stop by my class for a chat. Had I never gone in, I would have been just another scary eighth-grade teacher, or worse yet, another unknown adult. Now I was another adult on campus that they knew and with whom they could feel comfortable.

Recently there has been a lot of research that confirms students' need for many adults as role models. It is from this research that the idea of an advisory homeroom originated. The idea behind this type of a homeroom is that students can develop a relationship with other adults on campus. Along these lines, if teachers were to periodically switch classes with other teachers, they would constantly be getting to know more students. Most importantly, students would get to know them. The more students feel at home and comfortable with the adults at the school, the more they will look forward to coming to school.

Imagine the power of having teachers from upper grades coming to teach in lower grades for a day or two a year. This can create a very powerful bond between grade levels within a school, and can also be powerful in creating bonds between schools. If the high school freshmen teachers came to visit eighth grade, it wouldn't be as scary for the students to move up. If the sixth-or seventh-grade teachers visited the elementary schools, it wouldn't be as hard for the younger students to enter junior high.

As an eighth-grade teacher, there is no way that I can effectively prepare my students for the ninth grade when I have never been to the high school. It is similar to giving directions to a place that I've never been. I could probably read a map, and give the street names and where to turn, but I couldn't warn them about any potholes, suggest landmarks, or warn of the signs that are hard to read, because I wouldn't know about them.

Upper and lower grade teachers could trade classes for a day. The teacher moving up gets an opportunity to see former students and gets a feel for the climate in the next grade or school. By going to the classes himself, a teacher can come back aware of where his students are going and be better equipped to give accurate information to the students. Not only is this beneficial for the teachers, but it can help the students be more prepared to move on.

The teacher that goes to the lower grade benefits as well. She may begin to develop a long-term relationship with her future students. She can relay her expectations for behavior and the students can get a feel for her teaching style. This exchange could be done easily at all grade levels. There is no need to call a substitute, because there are good qualified teachers in both classrooms. If there is more than one teacher in the grade level above or below, arrange an exchange with all of them. It can do nothing but benefit all involved.

The ideal situation, of course, is to have the teacher actually go and teach at the different grade level for a few days a year, but a visit would also be effective. That, however, would require that a substitute be called, and some special arrangements be made.

Regardless of the way it is done, teachers need to spend time in grade levels above and below their own. This can even be extended so that teachers are visiting two or three grade levels below the one that they teach. The more student contact and the more the students know the adults at the school, the better.

A word of caution for those who see this as potentially valuable as I do. When I first began to do my visitations, I didn't tell any teachers except the ones that I was coming to visit. This was not done to hide anything—I just didn't see a need. However, I work in a school that has teaching teams. Parents can request teams, which sometimes creates a problem. Teachers that are better liked or known by the students end up getting requests. Usually, its the superior students that have the parents who care enough to do the requesting, so the teams can become unbalanced. There was a lot of resentment generated when I went out to meet my future students, because it was *perceived* as recruiting.

Before a teacher begins an exchange or visitation program, she must be sure that all fellow teachers are informed of her purpose and actions, and that they have a clear understanding of her intent.

Ideally, teachers at all grade levels would participate. Imagine the sense of community that could form if all the students knew who all the teachers were, and all the teachers were at least familiar with all the students. This sense of community could even be developed at schools with a thousand students, like mine. There is power in familiarity, and a wonderful sense of belonging when neither the students or the teachers feel lost in the crowd.

The Product

Feedback

A relationship with students before they get to the classroom is a great way to get to know the supply of students. Yet how do teachers know that their efforts have truly been effective beyond their classroom? Has the teacher prepared the students well for the next grade level? How would teachers measure it if they could? The product that teachers produce is the students' learning. Manufacturers use companies like JD Powers to give customer satisfaction surveys. Do educators ever ask their most valuable customers, their students, if they received the education that they came for?

Usually the only indication a teacher has that he has done a good job is when a student drops by for a visit, or during a chance meeting at a grocery store. Even then, the conversation is usually, confined to "How are you doing in school?", "Are the kids this year as good or bad as we were?", and "Gee, you sure have grown." In order to affect real changes in the classroom, the students need to be asked how well the teachers prepared them and what they could have done better. This discussion needs to occur in a productive setting where there can be open and meaningful conversation. Neither of the casual situations mentioned would work or be appropriate.

The first year that a teacher decides to ask for feedback, it may be a little tricky getting in touch with students that were in her classes. If the students are in the same school it's easy; if they've gone on to high school or college, it's a little tougher. When a teacher knows that she is going to request feedback each year, she should make sure to keep the contact records of the students that she wants to contact. I recommend that the teacher choose a wide variety of students in terms of behavior and academic performance. Students that were difficult in class are often really neat people outside the classroom. If the teacher has treated them with respect, they will usually be willing to come and give quality feedback. One such difficult student came to visit the year after he left and helped confirm what I believed. I never just sent him to the office, but consistently worked with him to help improve his behavior. He said to me, "I've turned things around now that I'm in high school largely because, even though I gave you a hard time, I never felt talked down to or disrespected." That little piece of feedback has given me new strength when continuously working with some students that don't seem to be improving. That student showed me that the payoff may come later than I want, but it will still come.

The students that have great behavior and high academic achievement are usually very excited at the chance to give feedback. Once it's known that this is a regular part of a teacher's program, students often ask if they can be the ones to get called the next year. If no one is willing to come back and talk, that in itself is feedback.

Contacting students from previous classes can be a wonderful experience. Teachers get to meet with the students in an informal setting and talk to them openly and honestly about their programs and how they helped them prepare for the next grade. After the first quarter of the school year, my teammate and I called about 10 of our former students for an informal get-together at a local pizza place for free food. (This ensures that the boys show up.) The students that we have contacted have been very receptive to the opportunity to talk and share their insights. It makes them feel special that a teacher values their feedback enough to seek it out. We usually call them and set up a mutually convenient time after school or in the early evening. It is good to contact the students after the first quarter, so that they have a solid feeling about the new school or grade. This also ensures that they have experienced some level of success or failure.

When we met with the students for the first time, we wanted to get an evaluation of how we did in preparing them for high school. After the normal greetings, we did a Plus Delta chart (described fully in chapter 8). We did the positive side first. This is a wonderful time of celebration for teachers, as they hear what they did well.

Then we asked the students to tell us how we could have been better. *Warning*: Teachers will probably hear things about their programs that didn't help or may have even hindered the student's progress. This cannot be a time to have a sensitive ego. Teachers focused on improvement are looking for ways to improve, so if there is something in their programs that is detrimental to the students' progress, no matter how much they may be attached to it, it must be stopped. The students are usually very honest, and don't bring it up unless it made a difference.

This is the feedback that teachers desperately need. They may believe that their programs are doing wonderful things, yet if the students aren't seeing the benefits, what good are they? On the other hand, it may be a time of wonderful validation if their programs do exactly as they intended. Usually it is a mixture of both. The teachers that can maximize the pluses and change the negatives will continually produce better students, and society in general, the ultimate customer, will benefit the most.

Our team is working toward meeting with the students four times in a year to continually get updates and feedback about how our program helped them, and how we can better prepare our current students for high school. Sometimes the students bring their current work to us. In one case, a girl brought some work that showed that the high school English teacher was teaching essay writing in a completely different way than she had learned in eighth grade. In fact, what she had learned in the eighth grade was of absolutely no use to her in her current class. As a result, these English teachers are beginning to work on a way to support each other better.

It was also in one of these discussions that I discovered that the freshman science program was nearly identical in content to the eighth-grade program. Without the student feedback, this may have never been detected.

Mentors

Once the teachers have discussed with former students how to improve their programs, a logical next step is to see if the students would be willing to come to their classes and help prepare the current students. There is real power in students telling other students, especially younger ones, what is needed to succeed or even survive at the next grade level. They can advise them on what they really need to do, know, and expect, and on the real consequences of their choices. I have also begun to use them to help current students with projects.

One of the big projects that I do in my class is the Mars Colonization. The students are required to use the scientific knowledge that they have acquired in astronomy and the knowledge they have acquired in history to build a colony of the future. It is a very complex project that takes one and a half to two weeks to complete. I have former students come in and help the current students solve the various challenges that they encounter while attempting to set up their colonies. Since my previous students have already resolved these challenges, they know what questions to ask and how to solve the problems that the current students have.

The students I ask to come help are invited based on the type of people that they are. Obviously, it would be unproductive to have students that behave inappropriately in the class, so I'm selective. Once the mentors are trained in what I want them to do, it is like having a few of me all over the room. And the mentors love doing it. One student commented after the experience was over, "Now I know why you teach the way you do. I got to go around and pose questions to kids to make them think all day and it was really fun!" The current students benefit as well. They don't have to wait for me to finish helping other students; they can get help right away.

The mentors can help with a variety of things. They can put together mini workshops to help the current students be more prepared for high school. They can help the current students with reports, labs, and so forth. Having them there brings a real sense of extended family to the classroom and it catches the current students' attention. The current students always ask if they can be mentors next year. The mentoring program can even be extended to include students from two or three years earlier. Recently, I had students from last year's class and a class two years before helping my current students on a project. Not only does this benefit the students academically during the current school year, but it can also help them socially when they get to high school. Having worked with high school mentors already, they may see some familiar upper-class faces and not feel as lost in the crowd when they get there.

The classroom is a system in itself, but by working the system that the class is in, there are huge benefits and resources to both the teachers and the students!

Key Points

- The classroom is a system. It is important for teachers to identify the parts of the system within and outside the classroom.

- Students play a multifaceted role in the classroom. They can be looked at as the supply, the customer, and the product.

- It is very important to work closely with the suppliers and the customers outside of the classroom.

- It is possible to create relations with the supply of students before they come to the classroom.

- Exiting students, the product of the system, are mentors and important sources of feedback.

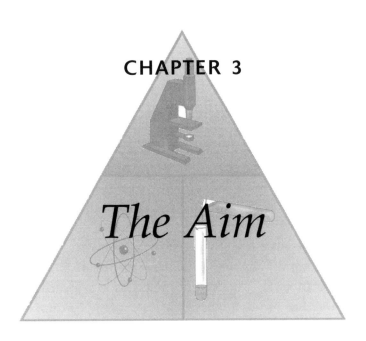

CHAPTER 3

The Aim

"The first step in improvement is agreement upon a common aim."

W. EDWARDS DEMING

Deming's First Point (adapted for the science classroom)

Create consistency of purpose toward improvement of the students and the teaching, with the aim of producing knowledgeable students who can compete in the global marketplace.

When W. Edwards Deming was hired by a U.S. auto manufacturer to help turn the company around, the first thing he did was ask what their aim was. They did not have an answer. He sat back and said that there was nothing he could do for them until they had an aim. Many of the executives were angry. They were paying him lots of money to consult with them, but now he refused to do anything. It forced them, however, to really look hard at what the aim of the company was. In what direction did they want to go? The aim of making cars with the newest technology can be very different from making a car that pleases the customer. Deming was right. Before any improvement could be made, they had to decide what they wanted to accomplish.

The importance of having an aim in the classroom is also very important. It becomes the guiding light and the focus of the classroom through the year. It also becomes the gauge by which activities and projects are selected.

I assume most teachers are like me. I had a vague direction in my mind for many years, yet it was difficult for me to communicate what I believed. If asked, I would need 15 to 20 minutes to explain my philosophy. I said much more than necessary and, in the end, I wasn't sure if I had really communicated anything at all.

What is the aim of science education in general? Is it to produce a nation of physicists, biologists, and/or chemists? Is it to produce people that have a general knowledge of all subjects? Are students to memorize facts about science, or are they to leave school with a knowledge of how things work? These questions, and others, need to be answered because these answers will define the aim of science education. This aim will then dictate how teachers teach.

State frameworks often give a general aim for the state's teachers to follow. It seems that states fluctuate between memorizing facts for standardized tests and having the students be "science literate." But what does "science literacy" mean? The science department at my school summarized the definition of "science literacy" from our state framework. It includes

- Developing positive attitudes in students about science and taking an active interest in natural phenomena and technological applications.

- Understanding scientific concepts and how they apply to daily living.

- Developing scientific thinking processes for lifelong learning.

- Developing positive attitudes and knowledge about science so as to live as an informed citizen in a technologically advanced nation.

Once we listed the main points, we put them into a statement that could serve as the aim for the department. For example:

Parsons Junior High Science Department will develop students' positive attitudes about science through activities that relate to natural phenomena and their applications in daily life. Teachers will foster techniques and thinking processes that help to develop the students into lifelong learners who can live more productively as citizens in a technologically advanced nation.

This example shows a brief statement that communicates what the teachers could stand for in the science department at Parsons. They would focus primarily on *developing positive attitudes, applying science to daily life, and fostering thinking processes.*

But what about the individual classrooms? Should they have the same aim, or should each individual teacher have an aim for her class? It really doesn't matter as long as the classroom aim, if unique, supports the department aim. Having unique aims allows the teaching team's or individual's personality and style to show through.

Recently, through a change in administrative philosophy, I began teaching with a new interdisciplinary team of teachers. At our first meeting, it was important to know where each of us stood and how each of us would run our classrooms. So we each set out to write down our own aim. It was harder to do than I thought.

Writing my aim was an incredibly complicated and valuable process. It forced me to think very carefully and thoroughly about exactly how I wanted my classroom to be. First I recalled the definition of an aim:

An aim is a concisely written statement of the purpose of the classroom. It should convey the major themes that will run throughout the activities, not the ways in which they will be accomplished.

I tried to focus on big ideas. My first draft read like this:

The aim in Mr. Burgard's science class is to produce students that not only acquire skills and know how to apply them, but also see the interrelationships of all things and subject areas.

The first aim I wrote didn't exactly match the vague aim in my mind, so I began to play with the language. The component on which I wanted to elaborate had to do with the last part of the statement. I'm passionate about doing interdisciplinary work and helping the students see the relationship among curricular areas.

A later draft read like this:

By using science to explain and understand their world, students will develop an appreciation of natural things and an understanding that will allow them to apply the information that they have gained. Students will also see and understand the role of other classes in science and become aware of the impact science has had on the past and will continue to have on the future.

This said more of what I wanted it to say, yet it was very complicated. I needed to keep it simple, direct, and concise. After many revisions, readings, and frustrations, I finally was pleased with this one:

Students acquire information to understand and apply their knowledge to the world around them, while increasing their enthusiasm and awareness of the impact science has on the human condition.

It took tremendous revision and thought to get the aim to say just what I meant. Yet in the end it was well worth it. This final version was the twenty-fourth or twenty-fifth try. Sometimes the challenge was the search for one or two words that would cover many thoughts. For example, I decided to use the words "human condition" to refer to humans past, present, and future.

I work in a team. After we came up with our own individual aims, we met to compare them, and to come up with a team aim. To find a team aim, we looked for similarities in our individual aims. Once we found where we thought alike, it was easier to construct a team aim.

Here are the aims from the other teachers.

HISTORY

To guide the students into understanding the relevance of history as it relates to their lives and to situations in the world today.

LANGUAGE ARTS

To understand and implement communication through reading, writing, speaking, listening, and thinking. To recognize and use these skills in all areas of life.

MATH

To develop the skills necessary to excel in a continuously changing technological society.

We found the most common idea from our aims was the desire to be interdisciplinary and find applications to real life. This then guided our thinking in writing a team aim. This is what we decided on:

TEAM USA

Use the lessons of the past to create a better future.

When each teacher has a personal aim that fits into a bigger team aim, the parents and the students can have clear expectations. These individual and team aims need to work in conjunction with the department, the school, and even the district aim, if these exist. Where I work, we have both a school and a district aim. Each aim is a little broader than the last, and shows how a system can be represented by each of the component parts.

Here are the aims in ascending order.

SCIENCE CLASS AIM

Students acquire information to understand and apply their knowledge to the world around them, while increasing their enthusiasm and awareness of the impact science has on the human condition.

TEAM USA AIM

Use the lessons of the past to create a better future.

PARSONS JUNIOR HIGH AIM

Parsons provides strong and effective academics and a safe environment while maintaining programs for student success and creating a sense of belonging and purpose for all students.

ENTERPRISE SCHOOL DISTRICT AIM

Maintain enthusiasm while increasing learning.

DEMING'S AIM FOR EDUCATION

To increase the positives and decrease the negatives so that all children keep their yearning for learning.

Once the aim has been established it stays the same. Now the goals and objective can be set forth to accomplish that aim. Goals are the big steps toward the aim, and objectives are the steps to achieve those goals.

A ship that sets sail with no aim will surely arrive somewhere. The question, of course, is where? Teachers who have clearly defined aims for their classrooms let the students, the parents, the school, and the district know exactly where they intend to go.

Key Points

- The aim is the concisely written purpose of the classroom.

- Writing a classroom aim is a highly rewarding and eye-opening experience.

- The aim in the classroom should vertically align with the team, department, school, and district aims.

CHAPTER 4

Preparation for Continuous Improvement

Deming's Fifth Point (adapted for the science classroom)

Constantly improve every activity in the classroom, in order to improve the quality and production of the teacher and each student, while decreasing the likelihood of failure.

Once the classroom is viewed from a systems perspective, it is then time to get the classroom and students set up for continuous improvement. In my classroom, I do it in two simple ways: The Improvement Journal and The Improvement Board.

Continuous Improvement Journal

Over the last few years, the *improvement journal* has gone through many transformations. The improvement journal is a booklet given to, and maintained by, the students. It contains all of the personal graphs, charts, and information they need for tracking their progress. It also gives the parents a place where they can see how their child is performing. I work with four other teachers in an interdisciplinary team, so the improvement journal that we have contains information for all the classes within it. For the purpose of this book, I will only go through the science section. There are four main sections to the science improvement journal. They are calendars, rubrics, a list of 100 facts, and run charts.

Calendars

The front of the journal contains nine blank calendars that the students can use to write down important dates for assignments or homework. It is a wonderful tool for communication with the parents. Many times a child will tell the parents that he has no homework. Then at the end of the quarter, the parent finds out that the student was lying. Some of the students in my classes are required by their parents to write down their homework assignments in the calendar each day. Then I initial the entries if they wrote them down correctly. By having it all in a journal, students don't have to keep track of a piece of paper that could get lost or misplaced.

Rubrics

The coming chapters will show how I train the students in my class to be able to evaluate themselves and their work objectively. I use rubrics that they keep in their journals to evaluate everything from written work to their behavior with a substitute. (These rubrics are explained fully in chapter 2 and chapter 10.) I don't want the way that I evaluate them to be a mystery, so I give them the tools that I use to grade them. No longer am I the one giving the grade. It becomes readily apparent that since they know exactly how they are being evaluated, they are choosing their own grades. They have rubrics for the following areas: Problem of the Week evaluation, substitute evaluation, partner evaluation, and assignment evaluation.

The Error Chart

Students use this chart to track the specific areas that they need to improve on. Its use is covered in depth in chapter 6.

The 100 Facts

The students are given the 100 facts that they need to know about science by the end of the year. This list and its uses are covered in depth in chapter 5.

Individual Run Charts

The students are given the tools to track their own improvement in four areas: acquiring information, acquiring knowledge, tracking enthusiasm, and tracking learning. This allows the student to know whether or not he is improving week to week and month to month. Parents can also use these run charts to check their child's improvement in performance and attitude throughout the year.

This journal can be put together in many ways. It can be given to the students as separate sheets of paper for storage in a section of their binders, or it can be plastic-spiral-bound in a complete and separate book. My team binds it into a book and gives each student her own copy the first week of class. The students are then responsible for keeping track of their own journals for the whole year. My teaching team calls these "Life Journals," because the student's whole eighth-grade academic life is contained within it.

Little Rewards

It's a lot of fun to get little sticker rewards for a job well done. Although this is definitely optional, teachers that work with junior high students know that they love stickers just as much as little kids. As a recognition for perfect scores, I give the students gold stars or blue ribbons to put on their journals. The gold stars are for a perfect 10 on the Weekly Ten facts quizzes described in chapter 5, and the blue ribbons are for a perfect 6 on the Problem of the Week described in chapter 6. The students do not work just for the sticker, but it is a small recognition of excellence. Also, when the class hits a total of 200 correct in the Weekly Ten facts quiz, I give them all stickers that say "200" on them. It is a way of recognizing everyone's efforts in reaching a common goal. Whatever method you choose to recognize their efforts, make sure it is small enough that it doesn't take away from the intrinsic motivation the program brings.

Continuous Improvement Board

The students' job is to keep track of their own individual improvement throughout the year. They keep track of their Weekly Ten quizzes, Problem of the Week scores, and enthusiasm and learning improvement. My job includes keeping track of the class improvement in a visible place on the wall. There are five things that I track on the Improvement Board. They are the class total for the Weekly Ten, the class total for the Problem of the Week scores, turn-in percentages for the Problem of the Week, substitute evaluations, and the enthusiasm and learning charts for each class.

Class Run Charts

I make two big charts to track the class totals in both the Problem of the Week scores and the Weekly Ten scores. On each laminated chart, the week number is on the horizontal axis and the number correct is on the vertical axis. Since I have five classes, I track all five on the same chart and use a different color for each. I went to the local office supply store and picked up five different colors of small sticky dots. Each week when the totals are calculated for the class, I put a sticky dot over the correct week and connect the dots with an overhead pen of the same color. (I laminate the poster and use overhead pen so that I can reuse the same graph the next year.) Since I do each class in its own color, the resulting graph is a colorful testimony to improvement. The students can see how their class is doing compared to the other classes, and also see that as a whole team there is improvement. I put a big dot on the graph to show how high last year's class got, and the current classes set out to beat it. This creates a little friendly competition that spurs students to do better for the benefit of the class and the overall team. For more on the class run charts, see Part 4 of chapter 5.

Unfortunately, the run charts can be deceiving. I had a class that beat the previous year's high score on the Weekly Ten in the 14th week of school. Their class was of comparable size, so they deserved the pride that they felt. That same week, another class pointed out that they could never beat the previous year's score. They were a small class. Even if they all got 10s, their totals would not beat the previous class's score. They suggested that I start keeping track of the *average* number correct per student, as well as the total correct. That way they might see more accurately how they compare to the other classes.

When I followed their suggestions, I realized the smaller class was scoring, on average, higher than the bigger class that beat the previous class's score. As a matter of fact, they had the lowest class totals and the highest average per student for many weeks in a row.

Another form of class run chart, shows the turn-in percentages of the Problems of the Week discussed in chapter 6. Each week at turn-in time, I have the students count and calculate the percentage of students who have turned the assignment in on time.

Problem of the Week Histogram

The Problem the Week Histogram provides a way to breakdown each class and the team into score catagories. It is a simple series of histograms, each having seven columns, one for each score 0 through 6. This series of graphs shows each problem of the week separately for comparison.

I put a color coded dot for each student on the correct score catagory. The color corresponds with the colors used by each period on every other chart and folder in the class. For example, this year my first period class was coded light blue on every chart and folder. So each first period student was represented by a light blue dot on the histogram. Each second period student was an orange dot, and so on. All the students get put on the same histogram each Problem of the Week, so that the students and I can see how each class, as well as the whole team, is performing.

Enthusiasm and Learning Graphs

On the board, there is one graph for each class that the students fill out to give me a feeling of how they perceive the class. Each class uses the same color dots that were used in the run charts described above. That way it stays uniform and easy to read. A full explanation of how the students fill these out and what to do with them is given in chapter 9.

Substitute Teacher Evaluation Graph

Each time there is a substitute, the substitute evaluates the class on a rubric that the students developed. Using the same color code as the two previous graphs, the students are evaluated and tracked for improvement in their behavior and cooperation. This rubric is explained fully in chapter 10.

This continuous improvement board can be arranged however a teacher wants. I have found that the graphs themselves, when visible to the students involved and all other classes, become motivators. This, combined with the individual achievements that they keep track of in their improvement journals, sets the stage for celebrating improvement in all areas of the class all year long.

Key Points

- It is important to set the stage for a continually improving classroom.

- Students need to be given the resources to track and evaluate their own improvement.

- A place in the classroom needs to be set aside to monitor class improvement.

SECTION 2

EPISTEMOLOGY

"The study or theory of the origin, nature, methods, and limits of knowledge."

Improving student learning.

Most of the student graphs shown in this section were produced on the computer program *Class Action* described in the preface. It makes keeping track of the data a little easier and produces great graphs, but is not required! The blank run charts provided in Figure 5.2 and Figure 6.8, and the blank error chart in Figure 6.10, are all that is needed.

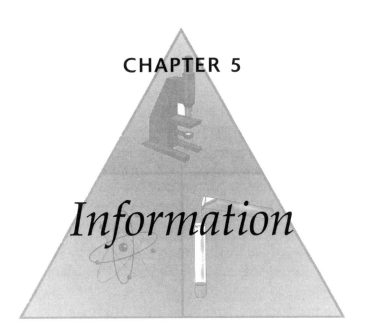

CHAPTER 5

Information

Part 1
Overcoming the Challenges of Retention

Most teachers face the challenge of how to give students both a maximum of hands-on experiences, and proficiency with the facts and skills that show they are educated for this society. Schools have been on a pendulum of ideas for years. There are schools and teachers that focus on skill with drill and repetition. Others take what is referred to as a whole language, or new math, approach that emphasizes understanding, with the hope that facts and skills will be acquired automatically. Some also attempt a balanced approach, yet find it difficult to really track growth, or to keep the information in the child's long-term memory.

Each method is worthless in isolation. The child who has memorized facts but cannot apply them, or doesn't have a deep understanding of them, is just as ineffective as a child who has enjoyed the activities, yet doesn't remember the facts and skills needed to tackle new challenges. There has to be a balance between experience and skills, and an easy way to monitor student progress.

I, too, have ridden the pendulum. I have taught science classes structured totally toward experience and hands-on activities. All the boys and girls loved it and could remember the information for the immediate test or to finish the project. Yet a month or even a week later, the information was gone.

Sometimes students had a great experience, yet *never* assimilated the information that the experience was supposed to convey. Once, when teaching the difference between chemical and physical changes, I presented many hands-on labs, and the students had a great time. They could even tell me the difference on the test, a day or two later. Yet when asked a week later, many could not remember. What happened? The activities were interesting, motivating, and applicable to real life, yet no information was retained. How could I convey the information and help the students develop the skills needed, without killing their enthusiasm by rote memorization or book work?

Now many states are incorporating mandated testing, and standards that students are required to meet. I believe that this accountability is going to be very good for the schools in the long term. Right now, however, it is a struggle as classroom teachers wrestle with changing the way they teach so that students do well on the standardized test. Teachers know that teaching "to the test" is both damaging to the students and severely limiting to programs. But poor performance on these tests *may* soon have unfortunate consequences not only for students, but for teachers' jobs as well. Is there a way to teach so that the test scores will improve, and the teachers can hang on to the integrity of their programs?

Although a shift in teaching will be difficult to make, it is necessary. The attitude that must be taken as the shift occurs ties into Deming's second point:

Deming's Second Point (adapted for the science classroom)

Adopt the new philosophy. We are in a new educational age. Public schools must awaken to the challenge, define their purpose, and set an example.

The institution of standardized tests was the result of a poor-quality product from the schools. The students of the last few decades have not retained their learning. When they reached the ultimate customer, business, they were ill prepared. Teachers understand that there is far more than the educational system to blame for this, yet the schools are the easiest and best scapegoat for the problem.

So the nation has responded in the only way it knows. It has incorporated mass inspection at the end, to try and force schools to produce a better product.

Putting mass inspection at the end of the process isn't suddenly going to change the quality of the product! And teaching "to a test," which most educators know doesn't show any real knowledge, would be a huge step backward. Yet this seems to be what teachers are being asked to do. Is it possible to jump through this hoop? Is it possible to teach deeper science and still have students "look good," on the standardized test? Yes! The answer is in *constant improvement*.

Deming's Third Point (adapted for the science classroom)

Cease dependence on inspection to achieve quality. Eliminate the need for mass standardized testing by building quality into the students in the first place.

I stumbled on the first step of this answer when reading Deming's ideas on the difference between *information* and *knowledge*. A chapter in Dr. Lee Jenkins's book, *Improving Student Learning,* provided the next step. It gave me a clue on how to use Deming's philosophy in a science classroom.

Information is that which has been learned in the past, such as facts and definitions. *Knowledge* is how to apply those facts to create a better future.

Part 2
Developing the List

It is first necessary to decide what *information* the students should have when they leave the class at the end of the year. The purpose of a final exam has always been to test the students' retention of the facts gained during the year. This is what standardized tests are supposed to evaluate. The students are required to gather facts through lecture and experience throughout the year. At the end of the year, they are tested on what they remember. When a student does poorly on a final exam or test, she blames the teacher and the teacher blames the student. One of the reasons the result could be poor is that some of the information required on the test hasn't been talked about for three or four months. The students and the teacher need a way to constantly review the information in a way that is not only effective, but exciting and motivating to the students.

The facts the students are supposed to know and remember from a particular class should not be revealed slowly throughout the school year. The information from the beginning of the year is forgotten and the information at the end of the year doesn't have time to sink in. Is there any reason students shouldn't be given, at the beginning of the year, the information that they will be required to know by the end?

At the beginning of the year, I give my students a list of the facts that they need to know by the end of the year. Since they are given all this information at the beginning, they can easily refer to it anytime. But how do teachers decide what goes on the list?

I developed the first list of facts off the top of my head while sitting at a conference. (Good ideas come at the strangest times.) I didn't want to check the validity of the list with my colleagues until I had actually tried to use it. I went quickly through all the curriculum I could remember and picked out what I thought to be the most important concepts and facts for the students to know. I was so excited that I quickly typed them up and gave them to my students so that I could start. The list was okay, yet definitely needed some work. Some of the statements weren't worded correctly, and I used no standard to make the list. At the end of the first year, I was convinced that the program worked, so I solicited input from my colleagues to improve the list.

The first thing we did was to create general categories for the facts. In our school the eighth graders study astronomy, heat, geology, chemistry, and genetics. Although it is not important to do, we decided to list the facts in the order that the students would receive them throughout the year. (See the list in Figure 5.1.)

Once the categories were set, we referenced our text books, state standards, district curriculum standards, and our own activities and experience. The number of facts that we needed was unimportant. It could have been any number. We chose 100 because it was a nice round number, and we could buy a 100-sided die, the use of which I will describe later.

The topics came more easily than the wording of the facts. The facts and concepts had to be written in a concise way, so that each was a statement that was easy to read and remember. The wording also had to coincide with how the students might receive it on a standardized test. Through countless changes, rewordings, additions, and deletions, six hours later we had our list.

The development of this list (which is by no means finished, and will be revised again next year) was one of the most valuable experiences I have had in designing what I teach. To focus on what I, the state, the district, and the school wanted the students to know, I had to look at the scheduled class activities in a completely different way. If the activities did not develop a deeper understanding of the facts that I was giving them, it would need to be either revised or thrown out. It gave me a whole new focus and direction. It didn't change *what* I taught; it altered *how* I taught it.

Astronomy

1. Stars are spinning clouds of gases that radiate heat and light through nuclear fusion reactions, changing hydrogen to helium.

2. Most astronomers believe the big bang theory of the universe, which states that the universe began with a great explosion of concentrated matter and energy and has been expanding ever since.

3. The spectrum of the light coming from the stars helps determine its temperature and composition.

4. Our sun is a medium-sized star.

5. Stars are made by the gravitational attraction of the gases in a nebula.

6. Stars have a life cycle. The way a star dies is determined by its mass.

7. Massive stars can turn into black holes, supernova, or neutron stars. Smaller stars cool to become white or brown dwarfs.

8. The closest galaxy to our own Milky Way is the Andromeda Galaxy.

9. Distances to stars are so great that they are calculated by how far light travels in a year, or "light years." Light travels 300,000 km per second.

10. The distance from earth to the sun is called an Astronomical Unit (au).

11. Galaxies are huge collections of billions of stars held together by gravitational attraction.

12. Current theory says that gravitational attraction is caused by a warp in the "space-time continuum."

13. The greater the mass of an object, the greater the gravitational attraction.

14. Escape velocity is the speed a rocket needs to travel to escape the gravitational attraction of a celestial object.

15. Elliptical orbits are caused by the combination of inertia and gravitational attraction of the object being orbited.

16. A solar system contains a star, comets, asteroids, planets, and moons.

17. Period of revolution is when one object travels around another. For a planet, one revolution is one year.

18. Period of rotation is one spin on the axis. For a planet, one rotation is one day.

Figure 5.1.   The 100 Science Facts.

19. The moon appears to go through phases because of a person's perspective from earth as the moon revolves. One side is always lit, but we can only see part of it depending on its position.

20. The phases of the moon are: new, crescent, first quarter, gibbous, full, gibbous, last quarter, crescent.

21. The seasons are caused by the relationship of the tilt of the earth's axis to its position around the sun.

Heat

22. Heat is the form of energy the causes the motion of molecules.

23. Cold is the absence of heat.

24. Heat always moves from warmer objects to cooler objects until they reach equilibrium.

25. Temperature is a measurement of the average speed of the molecules within a substance.

26. Conduction is the transfer of heat through a substance by direct contact of the molecules.

27. Convection is the transfer of heat through substances due to density changes within the substance.

28. Radiation is the transfer of heat through waves.

29. Specific heat is the amount of energy needed to raise 1 gram of a substance one degree Celsius.

30. Zero degrees Celsius is the freezing point of water. One hundred degrees Celsius is the boiling point of water.

31. Zero degrees Kelvin (minus 273 degrees Celsius) is absolute zero, the point where all molecular motion stops.

32. Substances that transfer heat easily are called conductors.

33. Substances that don't transfer heat easily are called insulators.

34. Heating causes most substances to expand. Cooling causes them to contract.

35. A substance exists as a solid, liquid, or gas depending on the motion of its molecules. Fast—gas, medium—liquid, slow—solid.

Figure 5.1.   Continued.

36. Changes in a substance's state occur when heat energy changes.

37. Freezing point is the temperature at which substances change from liquid to solid. Melting point is from solid to liquid.

38. Boiling point is determined by pressure, not temperature. When the pressure in the substance equals the pressure outside the substance, it boils.

39. Sublimation is when a solid changes directly to a gas.

40. Evaporation occurs when a substance changes from a liquid to a gas. Condensation occurs when a substances changes from a gas to liquid.

Geology

41. The earth is composed of the core and mantle and is covered with the crust, which is cracked into sections called plates.

42. The plates move because of convection currents in the magma of the earth's mantle.

43. Earthquakes are caused by the sudden movement of part of the earth's crust.

44. Earthquake energy is transferred though Surface (S)-waves, Pulse (P)-waves and Longitudinal (L)-waves.

45. Faults are cracks in the earth's crust. The four types are strike slip, normal, reverse, and thrust.

46. The focus point is the place along the fault where the earthquake begins.

47. The epicenter of the earthquake is the point on the surface directly above the point where the quake occurred.

48. The Richter scale measures the energy released during an earthquake.

49. Volcanoes are caused by subduction of the earth's crust, which heats, melts, and rises to the earth's surface.

50. Most sedimentary rocks are formed when sediments are deposited, compacted, and cemented.

51. Igneous rocks are formed when magma cools.

52. Slow cooling and evaporation can create large crystals. Fast cooling can make small crystals.

Figure 5.1.   Continued.

53. Crystals are a result of the repeating bonding patterns of the atoms that the substance is made of.

54. Metamorphic rock is formed when igneous or sedimentary rock is transformed by heat and pressure.

55. Minerals are inorganic, naturally occurring compounds in the earth.

56. Minerals have specific properties: crystal shape, cleavage, hardness, color, luster, streak, and density.

57. The major causes of erosion are water, ice, plants, wind, and gravity.

58. Soils are composed of minerals, microorganisms, and decayed organic matter.

59. The four major volcano types are plug dome, shield, strato, and cinder cone.

60. Fossils provide important evidence of how life and environmental conditions have changed.

Chemistry

61. Atomic number of an atom is the number of protons.

62. Atomic mass, or weight, is the number of protons plus the number of neutrons.

63. An atom is the smallest particle of an element and contains *protons* which are positively charged, *neutrons* which are neutral, and *electrons* which are negatively charged.

64. A stable atom has an equal a number of protons and electrons.

65. An ion is a charged atom with an unequal number of protons and electrons.

66. An element is the simplest pure substance.

67. A molecule is made up of two or more atoms.

68. A compound is a pure substance formed by combining two or more elements.

69. Compounds containing specific combinations of elements have identifiable properties and react in predictable ways. (Examples are acids, bases, salts, polymers, alcohols, amino acids, etc.)

70. Combining equal amounts of acid and base particles makes a solution neutral.

71. All matter has *mass* (the amount of matter), *weight, volume* (the space the matter takes up), and *density* (mass divided by volume).

Figure 5.1.   Continued.

72. Matter can be identified by its physical properties such as color, shape, and texture.

73. Chemical properties are the ways in which a substance reacts with another substance.

74. A physical change has occurred when there is a change in the physical properties, but the chemical properties remain the same.

75. A chemical reaction has occurred when both the physical and the chemical properties have changed.

76. Endothermic reactions have occurred when energy is absorbed and the product is cooler. Exothermic reactions give off heat and make the product warmer.

77. Synthetic materials are not found in nature and are made by using our knowledge of chemistry to transform raw substances into materials with desirable properties.

78. Synthetic materials can help reduce the depletion of some natural resources, reduce cost, and create better products.

79. The disposal of synthetic materials can create safety and environmental problems.

80. A solute is a substance that is dissolved in a solution. A solvent does the dissolving in a solution.

81. A solution is a mixture in which one substance is dissolved in another substance.

Genetics

82. DNA (Deoxyribo Nucleic Acid) is the chemical compound that codes for all life and is found in the chromosome of each cell.

83. Each species has a specific number of paired chromosomes in the nucleus of each body cell.

84. Genotype is the gene makeup of a specific trait. Phenotype is the physical appearance of a specific trait.

85. Homozygous means having the same genes for a trait. Heterozygous means having different genes for a trait.

86. Dominant traits are the traits that are expressed when one or two of the same gene are present. Recessive genes seem to disappear when only one of the same genes are present.

87. In codominance and incomplete dominance neither trait is dominant.

Figure 5.1.   Continued.

88. Genes are segments of DNA found on chromosomes.

89. In sexual reproduction, two parent sex cells, each with half the number of chromosomes, combine to form the offspring.

90. Traits carried on the X chromosome are sex-linked traits.

91. Genetic engineering is the process in which genes or pieces of DNA are transferred from one organism to another.

92. Plants reproduce sexually though pollination and fertilization.

93. A flower is the reproductive structure of the plant.

94. Fertilization occurs when a male sex cell joins a female sex cell.

95. In a flowering plant the stamen produces the pollen (the male sex cell), and the pistil produces the ovule (the female sex cell).

96. A seed is a fertilized ovule and can be found in fruits, nuts, and pods.

Technology and So Forth

97. Scientific knowledge and development are dependent on technological advances.

98. Technological advances have enabled humans to do complex operations, process large amounts of data quickly, extend our observations, and manufacture intricate devices.

99. Technological development is based on understanding scientific principles, the physical limitations of the materials, and the scope of our knowledge.

100. An *observation* is a record of what you see. An *inference* is a conclusion based on what you observe.

Figure 5.1.   Continued.

Part 3
Administering and Evaluating Information

Once the list has been developed, the students receive their copies. I give the students the list of all 100 facts on the first Friday of the school year. When I pass it out I tell them that they now have all of the facts that they will need to know in science this year. I love the responses. The first is confusion. The students look at each other, then me, then each other. This is something completely out of their experience. No one has ever given them at the beginning of the year all the things that they need to know by the end of the year.

Once the initial shock wears off, they begin to ask very interesting questions. "You mean all we have to do is study this and we'll know everything that we need to know?" Of course the response is "Yes." More bewilderment and scratching of heads. Many students have said, "Isn't that cheating if you already give us all the information?" What a concept! Studying all the information that you will need to know is now somehow cheating? Hey, if it makes them feel like they are getting away with something, all the better.

Then I tell them that I would like them to read through these 100 facts once each week so that it will serve as a preview for what is coming. I also tell them that each week, starting that day, they will be quizzed on ten randomly selected facts. This means that they will be quizzed on things they have never heard of at the beginning of the year. That's when I really get a reaction. There is an instant cry of unfairness. How could I quiz them on what they hadn't been taught yet? When the whining subsides, I gave them an example. The first year that I did this resulted in such a perfect example, I'll share it.

I rolled the 100-sided die and came up with number 96. They all looked at their lists to find it. Well, none of them knew that the word *homozygous* means "same kind of gene." Again they complained how unfair it was, because they didn't know it, but I simply responded with, "Now you do!"

There was some nervous laughter and some more unhappy sighs, but I asked them to trust me and we went on with that first test anyway. By coincidence, number 96 was rolled that day. At first I didn't realize that it was the one I gave in the example, but the students did. They all laughed and started writing the answer before I asked the question. When I read the question, I laughed with them. Even though they hadn't seen that fact until that day, most got the answer right.

It is important for the students to understand that these tests aren't graded as a normal test would be. I help the students to understand that they are not supposed to know all the answers in the first part of the year. If they did, they wouldn't need to be in my science class. The purpose of the random testing is to show and keep track of *improvement* in their acquisition and retention of the facts, not to find out if they can cram for an exam the night before and do well under stress. Once the students understand that they aren't expected to get 10 correct out of 10 each week, their defenses come down, and they relax and let their minds work.

I am looking for improvement over time. Each week is not important in itself, but the combined growth for all the weeks is important. Because the die is random, students will have some days when they know a lot, and other days when they don't. But are they growing over time? One student shared with me how she felt about the random testing. She said, "It seems the more times I miss a question the better I learn it, because each time I miss it, I get more determined not to miss the next time." Most teachers know that the most successful people are the people that have failed more times than anyone else. Babe Ruth may have been the home run king of his day, but very few know that he holds the major league record for strike outs too. Nice quotes say that "The road to success is paved with failure." Is the classroom structured so that the students can fail a lot and still do well?

Each week, I randomly choose 10 questions from the list and quiz the students. I choose 10 so that the students are quizzed each week on the square root of the total number of facts. If there were 200 facts, they would be quizzed on 14 or 15 questions per week. There are several ways to generate numbers randomly: You can buy a 100-sided die (available at a school-supply store or from a catalog), use a random number generator on your computer, or draw numbers out of a hat. As long as the questions are picked randomly, the method is effective.

Either the students or I roll the die. Once the students get started, they will all want to roll the die, so I have a different student roll for each question. The number that comes up is the number of the fact that will be asked. The lists of facts in their Improvement Journals are phrased as statements, so I simply change the chosen statement to a question. The question can be asked in different forms: multiple choice, fill in the blank, or finish the sentence.

I generally state the topic that the fact comes from and then phrase the statement as a question.

Example: The die rolls 6.

I say, "The category is astronomy."

Fact 1 says: A star is a ball of swirling clouds of hot gas, mostly hydrogen and helium.

I could ask the question in a variety of ways.

1. a star is a _____

2. a star is

   a. a burning ball of gas

   b. holes in the sky

   c. a piece of a planet

3. What is a star?

4. Stars are swirling clouds of hot gas. Which gases?

The teacher can phrase the question differently each time that its number comes up. It is amazing how much the students remember about the last time a particular question was asked. I usually will say the number of the question twice and say the question twice. Question number 6 came up quite a few times throughout the year. Sometimes I would completely change the question around and say "A swirling ball of hot gas in space is referred to as a what?" Many students, remembering, would say, "Hey, you asked that differently last time." They still knew the answer, though. Students should be able to come up with the answer no matter how the question is phrased. By the end of the year they will literally know these facts forward, backward, and inside out.

When the question is asked, the students write the question number on their pages. In the example given, they would write down #6 and then their answer. When all 10 questions have been asked and answered, the students go to their own lists and correct themselves. This reinforces the learning again. Since technically the quizzes aren't "graded," there is no reason for the students to be dishonest when checking their answers. The students are remarkably honest with themselves. They often ask for clarification about whether an answer is "close enough." The ensuing conversation explaining why it is, or isn't, is a very teachable moment.

Once the Weekly Ten becomes a regular routine, and a consistent day is chosen, the students anxiously anticipate it each week. This creates an unusual dynamic. I'm still surprised when it happens. Technically, the students are being tested each week on what they are supposed to know for the whole year, yet they actually like being tested! They know if they are having a bad day it won't kill them. It is them against themselves. Their focus is can they *improve* this week? Students are studying to better themselves, not cramming to pass a one-time test for a day and never see the information again. Sometimes, because I post the class totals (as I will describe later), they study and do better for the good of the class. The students begin to want to improve for a cause greater than themselves—the improvement of the entire class!

Some students gave me some great feedback on how they felt about the process. A student that really struggled academically and personally said, "It (the Weekly Ten) gives me a chance to look at what I'm going to learn throughout the year and say, 'Hey, I can ask myself these questions before the teacher asks me.' And, I want to study this stuff so that we can beat the other classes. It makes it fun but you learn at the same time." He is realizing that he is *learning through the evaluation* process, and he looks forward to improving.

These questions are chosen at random. The students will be quizzed at the beginning of the year on things that they have never heard of before. That's okay. When they correct their quizzes, they will read the statement that they had never heard of, and by reading it they will be exposed to it. When it comes up again they are apt to remember it. Also, the quizzes will keep bringing up topics that they have already learned and can answer easily. By touching on the information weekly, the students will probably see each question three to four times in a 39-week school year. By charting the number correct each week, they will see real growth in remembering the information. The information never goes away.

Another benefit to using this system is what it does for the teaching. As teachers progress through the year, the students will know more and more about topics before they formally study them. On more than one occasion, as we finished an area of study, I have seen students studying the facts on the next area. One student told me, "I'm studying the facts of what is coming, so that I won't be as confused when we begin to learn new things. I will already have an idea of what you are talking about."

At first, it scared me. If the students took the 100-Fact List seriously and knew the facts of a topic before we got to it, what was I as a teacher going to do? My job used to be conveying facts—now what? Something more wonderful than I ever imagined resulted. Since the students already had a good idea of the facts as we entered a new area of study, they became detectives, trying to figure out how the facts fit together. For example, if they knew that heat caused molecules to move faster, how did that explain that things expanded when they got warmer? In class discussions, it became normal to present a situation and say, "What do you know about what is happening? How does that explain what is happening? And, what can we do with that information?" It allows teachers to work up and through Bloom's Taxonomy without leaving the facts behind! Not only did they memorize the facts for a test, but also they learned what they could do with the facts that they were constantly being exposed to. That is knowledge! The way to evaluate knowledge is in chapter 6.

By using this method, many things can be accomplished. Not only are the students constantly being bombarded with new, current, and old information, but the information is aligned with the state standards! No more hoping that the students are picking up the information as the year goes by and then having the final inspection on test day. The teacher can now actually monitor quality all along the way. This is hard data that tells the teacher how each student is progressing toward the final goal of knowing all the information by the end of the year. I tell my students that I won't bother them about their weekly scores until I notice negative trends. These negative trends would show as either a constant decline in their scores, or flatlining at a low score. If a student continually gets 1s and 2s, I can tell that something is wrong. This is pretty easy to convey to the students. I ask them, "If you are lying in a hospital bed and the electronic device hooked to your heart shows a flat line, what does that mean?" They usually respond in unison, "You're *dead*!" I continue, "If I notice that your run chart says your brain is dead, I will revive you!" How to keep track and chart their scores is our next topic!

Part 4
Monitoring Retention

With the growing emphasis on accountability in public schools, there has to be a way to show that the students are learning. The random Weekly Ten tests, discussed previously, are charted each week and are a clear way of showing improvement. The data can be tracked in four ways: the student run chart, the class run chart, the scatter diagram, and the histogram.

Deming's Twelfth Point (adapted for the science classroom)

Students must be put in charge of their own continuous improvement and be motivated intrinsically so that they take pride in their accomplishments. Take away grading based on number of assignments turned in, and give the students criteria for high quality and help them to achieve it.

The Student Run Chart

Each week, after the Weekly Ten has been given and corrected, the students go to their Continuous Improvement Journals and open to their own run charts. On these charts the students track their progress each week by putting a dot in the box, above the week, the number they got correct (see Figure 5.2). The students love this, because inevitably they do improve. Of course, not all improve right away, but over time they do. The teacher really needs to put the emphasis on *improving*, not on that day's score. If a student gets a 3 out of 10 one week when for the previous three weeks he had been getting 1s, the 3 is cause for celebration. If the 3 is down from a previous high score, it is not the end of the world. It was a tough week and she will do better next time. Most importantly, with the focus on *continuous improvement*, the student sees that she is learning. This becomes an intrinsic motivation.

The student run chart also serves as a valuable conference tool with parents. Again, because it is a record of improving over time, the parents can see that their child is learning. If she is not improving, the teacher can then provide some suggestions.

I sit down and have a talk with students who don't seem to be improving. I make sure that they understand the way to study and to correct the quizzes, and I tell them that I will continue to watch to make sure that they are learning. Each student with whom I have done this has improved the following week. For some students, it just takes longer for the information to sink in. One student had been earning ones for many weeks in a row. He was a nonnative speaker of English, so I had the ELL teacher talk with him after I did. The next week he got a two, and he didn't get a three or below in consecutive weeks again. (See Figure 5.3.)

There will be those students that will take the 100-Fact List and try to commit it to memory right away. I originally thought that it would be my more advanced students that would attempt this first, but I was pleasantly surprised that I was wrong. The first person that scored a 10 was a special education

Weekly Ten Facts Scores

For:

Place a dot in each square of the score you achieved this week.

Score																																				
10																																				
9																																				
8																																				
7																																				
6																																				
5																																				
4																																				
3																																				
2																																				
1																																				
0																																				
Week	1	2	3	4	5	6	7	8	9	10	11	12	13	14	15	16	17	18	19	20	21	22	23	24	25	26	27	28	29	30	31	32	33	34	35	36

Figure 5.2. Blank student run chart.

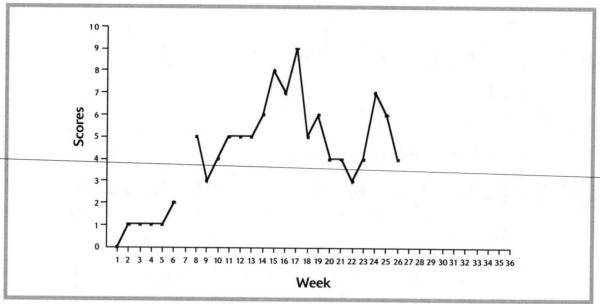

Figure 5.3.   Sample student run chart.

student. The rest of the class was as surprised as he was. When I asked him how he did it, he said, "Well you gave us all the information that we needed, so I just did what you said, and read though the list twice a week, and it just stuck in my head."

Another student that had Ds in most of his classes was also the first to get a 10 in his class. He said, "I just read the facts and think nothing of it, and after a while it gets into my mind and I memorize it. When it gets to the test, I just write it down."

A student may come in and say, "I've got the whole list memorized. "Well, first of all she would need to prove it. One perfect 10 does not show mastery. If a student gets 10 out of 10 for seven weeks straight, she is probably right; she has learned the list. According to statistics, after the seventh time scoring a 10 in a row, the likelihood that it is just luck is almost zero.

The probabilities work this way: The first time a student gets 10 out of 10 there is a 50 percent chance that it was luck. It could be that the only 10 that the student knew came up that week. The second time in a row that a student gets a 10, the odds of it being luck are 50 percent again, but it is 50 percent of the last 50 percent, or a 25 percent chance that it is luck. The third time a student scores a 10, the same thing happens, so there is a 12.5 percent chance. And it continues: 6.25 percent the fourth time; 3.125 percent the fifth time; 1.5625 percent the sixth time; and, finally, the probability that the seventh 10 in a row was luck is about 0.78125 percent. That's less that a one percent chance that it was luck. The student has then proved her point. The student can then mark the rest of her graph with 10s and do something else each week while the class does the quiz. Since she has marked 10 each week, her score still contributes to the total for the class even though she didn't take the test. This student could be put in charge of administering the test each week from then on, or doing the class totals and graphing.

I had my first student accomplish this seven 10s-in-a-row after the first 15 weeks. She felt, however, as though she still didn't know them all. She was honest with herself and knew that she had guessed and been right a few times. The guessing, although it helped her achieve seven 10s in a row, didn't necessarily reflect what she knew. She decided to continue to take the weekly tests for fun, even though she didn't have to. (See Figure 5.4.) There are a few of this kind of student every year.

Other students have gotten six 10's in a row and then scored a nine and had to start all over. The student in Figure 5.5 was one such student. Although it was frustrating for her, she committed the one she missed to long-term memory. She got 10s the rest of the year. This year, a student that had a similar thing happen to him came back from high school for a visit. I asked him if he still remembered the one that broke his streak. Not only did he remember the question and the answer, he even remembered what number it was on the list!

This same student came another day for a visit when the high school was not in session. It happened to be a day that we were taking the weekly test and he asked if he could also take it for fun. He took the test in each of three periods that day, so he was exposed to 30 different questions. He got 28 correct. That's long-term memory!

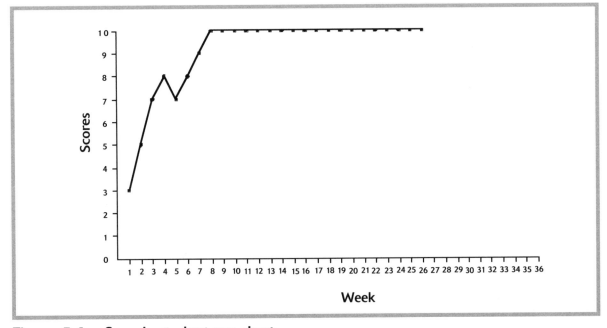

Figure 5.4. Sample student run chart.

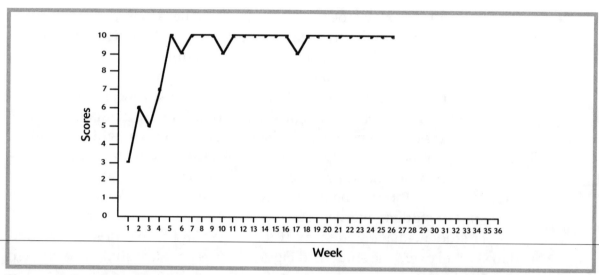

Figure 5.5.   Sample student run chart.

The next examples are of some students who don't normally do well in the classroom setting. The student in Figure 5.6 didn't do much work all year. He was in a very rebellious stage at home and at school, and figured getting poor grades would give him revenge. He was there, however, nearly every Friday for the Weekly Ten. This run chart shows that he grew a tremendous amount over the year. He was very vocal in telling his classmates when he improved his score.

The student in Figure 5.7 had never done well in school. He was a very nice kid but lacked many of the skills necessary to be an A student. Yet his run chart shows the growth that took place for him on the Weekly Ten. I'll never forget the look on his face when he finished correcting his ten and realized he got them all right. He held his head high the rest of the year. Although he dropped in later weeks, he still scored 5 or above the rest of the year.

These examples speak volumes about the intrinsic motivation that this program brings. These three students didn't improve because their parents and I wanted them to—they improved because it mattered to them. The learning became a byproduct of their desire to improve.

To help students keep track of which facts they know, and which ones would be beneficial to study, I have them highlight the ones that they get correct each week. They can use a colored pencil, highlighter, crayon, or whatever else they have that will shade, but not block out, the question. This gives them a great feeling of accomplishment as the 100 chart slowly, over the course of the year, is filled in. It also serves as a great study tool. Some of the students will take my advice and read through the questions weekly so that they may do better each week. If they know which ones they can skip and

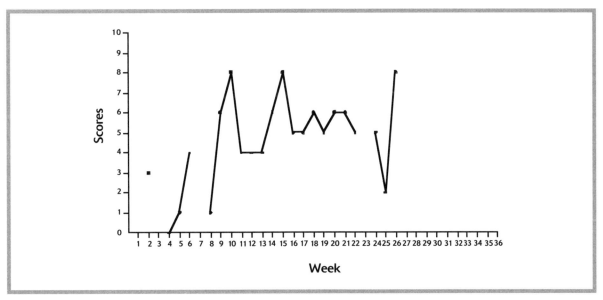

Figure 5.6. Sample student run chart.

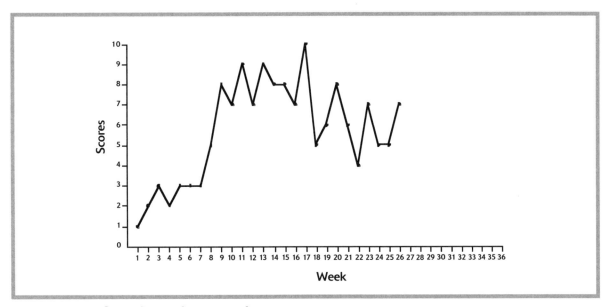

Figure 5.7. Sample student run chart.

focus on the ones they don't know, it will save them time. It is also another way for them to see their own growth, which leads to intrinsic motivation—the only true motivation.

The Class Run Chart

It becomes very exciting as the students record their own progress on the student run charts in their journals or binders. The teacher can track the class progress on the wall by counting the total number right for the entire class each week. I do this as a quick calculation by having the groups fill out Post-It notes, on which they write each group member's name and the number he or she they got correct. Each group then adds up its own total and the sticky note is given to me. The class is usually anxious to find out how they did, so we add the totals together as a class.

I set up an area in my class specifically devoted to tracking improvement called the Continuous Improvement Board (also described in chapter 4). I make one large chart that has the weeks across the bottom, and is numbered by fives from 0 to 320 on the left axis. I go to 320 because if I have a class with 32 students the possible total score for the class is 320. Since I teach five sections of science, I need to be tracking five sets of data. I can do this very easily on the one chart. For each class I choose a color. I then buy small sticky dots, a different color for each class. As the graph changes through the weeks, I connect the dots for each class with the same color pen as the dots. Eventually I have five line graphs that are constantly crisscrossing and showing improvement. (See Figure 5.8.)

The graph becomes an incredible motivation. The students wait with anxious anticipation each week as the points are added. Sometimes they are excited and happy because the graph went up, and other times they are not so thrilled because the graph has gone down.

The first week can be discouraging to a class. Totals can be as low as 40 to 50 correct out of 300 possible. Not exactly a great start, unless the teacher can use this as a teachable moment as well. Help the students to see from a different perspective. The start is just that: a start. What the teacher is looking for is improvement over time. If they already knew all the facts that the teacher was going to teach them, they wouldn't need to be there.

In an example of the long-term effectiveness of this technique, the first time I did this was in midyear. That meant that the students that year had already been exposed to approximately half of the facts on the list through regular

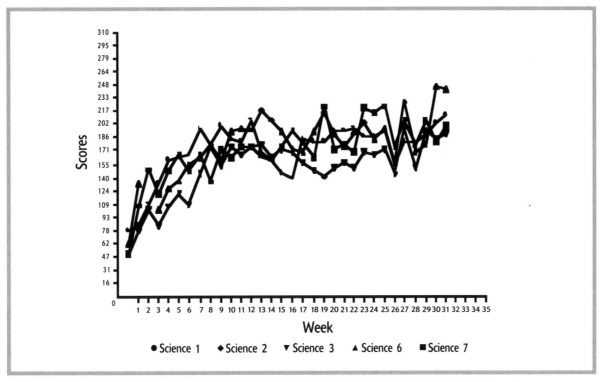

Figure 5.8. Combined classes class run chart.

teaching and testing when we started. Those students, however, scored no better on their first random test at *midyear* than students have scored on the first test at the *beginning of the year* every year since! The original students had retained almost none of the facts they had "learned" by midyear, yet most had done well on the unit tests when they were given. Classes now are easily scoring 180 to 200 or more correct by midyear. That usually gives an average of 7 to 10 correct for each student. What a difference!

Once the process starts, the students begin to become actively involved in their own goal setting, and in helping the class to improve. They can set a goal of getting at least a certain number correct for a given period of time and then celebrating when it happens. Or there can simply be improvement goals set so that the class decides it will get more correct next month than it did this month. A celebration takes place when the class reaches a new level of correctness, or when there has been consistent growth over a period of time. Everyone becomes involved. The student that gets only one right each week becomes a valuable asset to the class, because that one correct adds to the total correct each week for the class and therefore contributes to the overall success. Even a new student that knows nothing of what's been happening can be a help to the class.

I had a student arrive to class in April one year. The rest of the class had been doing the Weekly Ten for quite some time, so the poor girl felt a little intimidated. On the first Weekly Ten, she got one out of the ten right, and felt pretty stupid. That one point that she added, however, enabled the class to get its new high score of 235 out of 290 possible. She felt pretty good once she was told how the process works and that her score helped the class. The next week she got a three and continued to improve for the rest of the year. Although she only took the Weekly Ten for five weeks, on the fifth week she scored a seven and helped the class achieve 248 out of 290 for their final score.

There is a sense of competition that usually develops between the classes. This can be either a good motivator or a detractor. It's important to point out to the students that since that each class rolls a different 10 questions, there is really no comparison. Their only real competition is themselves.

With the class focused on improvement each week, it became apparent that a chart with only the total correct for the class each week wouldn't do. If students are absent, the individual scores might go up, but the class totals would go down. The students suggested that we take an average for the class each week. Good idea, but that means that half the class is below the average. So instead we decided to normalize the graph—we would see what percent of the total number of possible were correct. For example: if 28 students are present, there are a possible 280 correct. If the class got 200 correct, they got 71 percent correct. Look at the differences between the regular run chart in Figure 5.9 and the normalized graph in Figure 5.10. Many of the ups and downs of the improvement process are taken out and real improvement is easily seen.

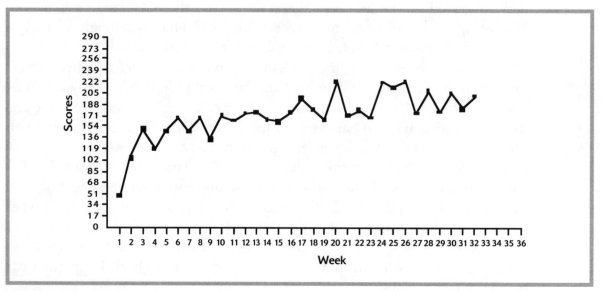

Figure 5.9.   Individual class run chart.

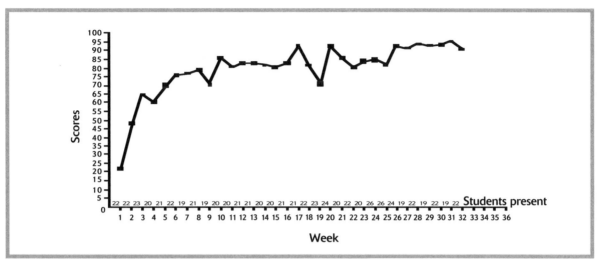

Figure 5.10. Normalized class run chart.

The Scatter Matrix

This next graph, shown in Figure 5.11, is mostly for my own interest, but could be shared with the class. It is called a *scatter matrix*. A scatter matrix is very useful when looking for trends. With this graph, the teacher can see *how many* students are getting each score and can get a more in-depth look at the class's improvement. Each dot above the week stands for one student who achieved a certain score. For example, if you draw a line straight up from the marking for week 2, the dots to the left of the line show that there were 26 students present. Their scores were pretty low with four 4s, ten 3s, six 2s, three 1s, and two zeros. However, by week 14, there was a big improvement. This time there were six 10s, ten 9s, two 8s, four 7s, and four 6s. This graph effectively shows the gradual upward trend toward 10s and the decreasing number of students who score below 3.

This is a great graph to use when the class totals drop. Compare the Class scatter matrix in Figure 5.11 with the Individual class run chart in Figure 5.9. Even though the class totals dropped in week 10, some of the individual scores went up. There were fewer 10s, but there were more 4s, 5s, 6s, and 7s with no 3s at all. Comparing the graphs is a wonderful way to check for common cause or special cause variation. Variation is covered in depth in chapter 7.

Another graph that is very useful at conference time is the *scatter matrix with student overlay*. This graph shows the student's individual run chart laid over the scatter matrix of the class. This allows a teacher or parent to see right where the child is performing in relation to the class. Parents often wonder

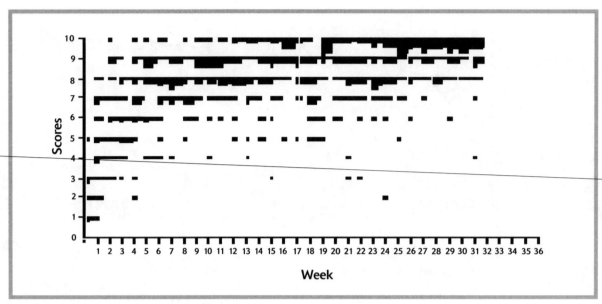

Figure 5.11. Class scatter matrix.

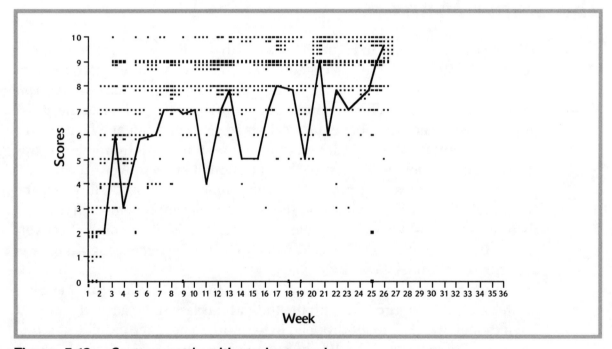

Figure 5.12. Scatter matrix with student overlay.

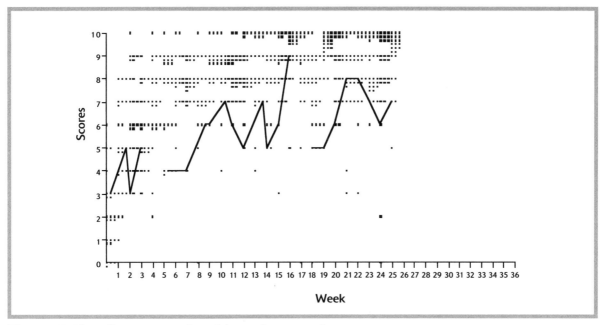

Figure 5.13. Scatter matrix with student overlay.

how their children compare. Figure 5.12 shows a student who has kept pace with the class improvement by staying right near the middle of the graph the entire time. Figure 5.13 shows a student who, although improving, is still trailing the majority of the class. Parents can walk away with a clear view of how their children compare, without ranking children. Improvement is the focus, and the children accomplish that.

The Histogram

The fourth and final way that data can show improvement, is through the *histogram*. The histogram allows teachers and students to look at improvement in chunks of time. This allows data to be analyzed on a quarter-by-quarter or semester-by-semester basis. In Figures 5.14, 5.15, and 5.16, histograms are used to compare first-, second-, and third-quarter performance of a class. Each graph provides cumulative totals for the entire nine weeks. For example, Figure 5.14 shows the cumulative score for the students in a class for the first nine weeks of school. There is only one student whose cumulative score—all nine scores added together—only reaches between 19 and 27 correct. On the same chart, there were seven students whose cumulative score was between 37 and 45 correct.

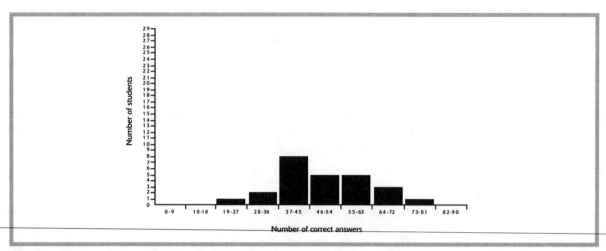

Figure 5.14. Class histogram for first quarter.

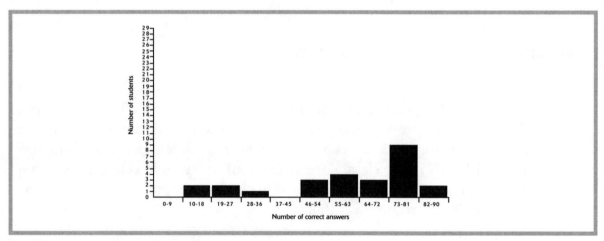

Figure 5.15. Class histogram for second quarter.

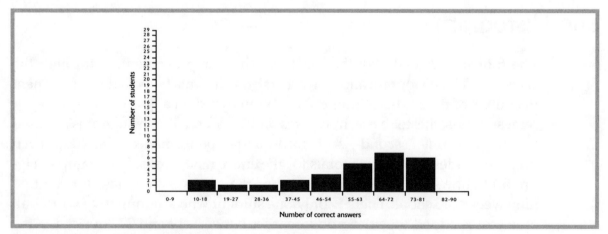

Figure 5.16. Class histogram for third quarter.

Compare that data with Figure 5.15 and you can see there has been a definite shift of scores to the right. These are the cumulative scores for the third quarter of the same year. Now there are 18 students whose cumulative scores are over 57, while there were only 4 in the first quarter. Students and teachers alike can easily see improvement. The histogram is one more tool that can be used to display data in the quest for improvement.

More Possibilities and Benefits

This data collection could become especially powerful when, rather than one teacher in his own classroom doing a Weekly Ten and keeping track of the data, the whole grade level decides on the list of facts and all the classes do it each week. Combining the expertise, standards, and curriculum of each teacher at the grade level and coming up with what students should know when they leave is a very powerful tool to create unity among the teachers as they work toward a common aim. The entire sytem would be working in unison!

It would be even better if it could be done across all the grade levels within the department, so that each grade had its own agreed-upon list. The students would be familiar with the program and anxiously anticipate the years 100 Facts. It would help to clearly define what the students should know at each grade level and in turn bring about true departmental unity. The students would see that there really is a system in place that extends beyond the individual classroom.

Remember, this process is only for keeping track of fact acquisition and *information*. It is not the only way that these facts are taught. Each individual teacher can use whatever activities he has designed to give experiences that will now serve to reinforce and provide a deeper understanding of the information that the students are seeing each week. This process literally changes the role of the teacher. Now, because the students become aware of the facts in advance of the unit, the teacher can plan activities that stimulate higher-level thinking.

The first full year I used this program I had an unexpected problem. It was a problem only because I was unsure how to work with it. My students were so motivated to learn the facts and improve their scores that I feared they would know the facts before we got to the labs I had created to help them discover these facts. Students can't very well "discover" something that they already know. They would not, however, have any background to give continuity or context to the facts. I had to restructure the class and the labs in terms of weaving the facts together, not discovering them. I had my more advanced students design their own experiments to prove or disprove the facts, while the other students would explain how the lab they had done confirmed or refuted the facts that they now know. The students actually become detectives, putting the pieces of information together to discover the story behind them.

If, after a teacher uses this evaluation system, an official or administrator comes to his room and asks for proof that his program is effective, he could show a mountain of data reflecting the continuous improvement in learning in his classroom. Then the accountability of teachers would no longer be an issue, and they could get on with their teaching! Not bad for a system of evaluation that students look forward to and enjoy.

Remember that the students do need to know this information by the end of the year. Each Weekly Ten quiz is a practice for the end-of-the-year final. We don't do the standardized test in science in our school yet, so I give them a 100-question, multiple-choice final at the end of the year that does count! One student asked, "Why?" I told him, "After all this practice, if someone doesn't know at least 65 percent of the facts for this class, they don't deserve to pass." He agreed.

Yet how can a teacher be sure that the students truly get the deeper meaning, now that they have the information memorized? The truly important things, the things that the standardized bubble in tests can never evaluate, is whether or not students can actually apply the new information in a real setting. Could the students teach the concept to someone else, and could they really use the information if necessary? Could they now take that information and do something with it? How to find and track student *knowledge* about a subject is discussed in the next chapter.

Key Points

- Students have a difficult time remembering facts that are learned for only one-time tests.

- Students should be given all the facts that they need to know at the beginning of the year.

- Those facts should be developed based on district, state, and national testing standards.

- These facts should be tested randomly each week to serve as a preview and review of the material all year long.

- Students can track their own improvement and goal setting while the teacher tracks class improvement and goal setting.

- This method becomes an intrinsically motivating force in the classroom.

- With the facts taken care of, more time can be spent on higher-level thinking.

CHAPTER 6

Knowledge

Part 1
Developing the Problem
of the Week

The Weekly Ten information quizzes discussed in the previous chapter are wonderful because they take some of the pressure off the teacher in the area of teaching *information*. The students will begin to come to class with the facts; the teacher's role then shifts from "bringer of facts" to "facilitator of knowledge."

According to Deming's theory of *profound knowledge*, knowledge is what is necessary to create a better future. It is a way of (1) relating the past to current events; (2) problem solving; and (3) experiencing the scientific method. If the students have the facts that they need to know, then the time in the classroom can be spent asking deep probing questions and finding out what to do with those facts. It is the "So what?" When done correctly, the students will no longer be able to ask "When are we ever going to use this stuff?" because that's the point of the whole class.

The Weekly Ten quizzes cement into their long-term memories the facts the students need to know, whether they want them there or not. Each quiz actually serves as a study tool. It forces the students to study, each week, all of the information for the year without knowing they are being forced to continuously review. To the teacher and student, the benefits of this whole-year preview and review don't really begin to show up until toward the end of the first quarter. By then, the students start to realize that these facts are helping them to understand the concepts they are studying. They start to read through the facts in their spare time. I approached a student I will call John one day as he was reading through his facts in class. I asked him, "Are you reading all of the facts?" He said, "No. I know that we are studying heat next, so I'm memorizing the heat facts now, so that I will have a better idea of what we are talking about when we get there." What a great idea! He started studying before we got to a topic, so that he would be more informed in the discussions that he knew that we would have. John was becoming a detective. He knew that he had the facts; now it was time to put together the story.

By midway through the year, lecture time is no longer used to convey facts. Now it is a time of detective work. Most of my discussions and labs are based on the premise that the students already know the facts.

For example: When we started to study heat, the class already knew that heat causes molecules to move and things to expand. So the lab I used to show that fact became a lab showing that, with expansion and contraction, we could also find absolute zero (which they also already knew was minus 273°C). It is not enough to know the facts; students must know how to apply them.

Now, how can a teacher easily and effectively evaluate that kind of knowledge in a way that both reveals the depth of student knowledge and tracks improvement? I asked the students to explain how they could demonstrate or prove that they knew something. They decided that, in order to truly demonstrate that they knew something, they would have to be able to teach it to someone else, or be able to do it in a different setting than the one in which it was learned. This kind of knowledge cannot be judged on a true/false or multiple-choice test. Not even a short-answer test could provide insight into this kind of awareness. Knowledge has to be evaluated the way a gymnast is scored in a competition. The gymnast may know all the skills "in the book," but if she cannot put them together into a routine that flows and shows mastery, she just knows isolated skills.

The first part of a knowledge evaluation idea came in my first year of teaching science. By the third quarter, I was very unhappy with the way I was evaluating the students. The tests I wrote never seemed to be anything but tests for facts. So, at the end of a unit on heat, I told the boys and girls that they were to remember all of the things that we had studied about heat and put them together into an essay called the "Story of Heat." I told them that the facts needed to be written in the essay form that they had just learned in their language arts classes, and that they had to really tell me what they understood about heat. The resulting essays showed me what they truly understood better then any test I had given.

Now, essay exams are nothing new. What I'm proposing is a modification of that proven idea. I call it the "Problem of the Week." The students generally refer to it as their "POW," so I will as well. The POW asks the students to review all the facts and labs that they have been studying the previous week and either explain, teach, or problem solve. They must use the information that they have gained, either to reteach a topic or to figure out a realistic situation. The POW turns the students into detectives, using facts to solve a mystery. The question usually requires the students to revisit labs, notes, and activities that they have done in order to answer the question. For example, when we began geology, we did many activities and had videos and lectures that helped the class to understand how tectonic plates move, and how and where earthquakes occur. This was the POW that I gave them:

 Use your knowledge of plate movement and earthquakes to describe why and how earthquakes happen. Describe the ways that plates interact. Then tell why there are so many earthquakes in California and not as many on the East Coast and in the central part of the United States.

This question required the students to know not only the facts about why and how earthquakes occur, but also to use that knowledge to explain their own environment.

Here are a few more examples.

 The last week we have been doing experiments with solutions and how to mix them. Have your mom buy a powdered drink mix, and mix a 10 percent solution. Describe, and show in detail how you made your solution 10 percent using the word solute and solvent correctly. Then describe the physical properties of your solution. Is it a true solution? How can you tell? Is the drink more concentrated, or more dilute than when you mix it by its real directions? What is the percent concentration when you mix it with the actual directions?

When I asked this question, most students had no idea that they could actually make a solution outside of the classroom. And they definitely didn't realize that they actually made solutions at home all the time.

Near the beginning of the 1800s, a man named Benjamin Franklin invented the first wood stove, called the Franklin stove. Now there are wood stoves in many homes across America. Use the knowledge you have gained about heat transfer to explain why many people prefer wood stoves over conventional fireplaces to heat their homes in the winter. (Be sure to use the words "convection," "conduction," and "radiation" properly.)

One of the things that I do with these problems is try to tie the science information and knowledge into the other subject areas. I do a lot of ties with history. Most scientific advances radically changed the path of history. Since in my school the eighth grade studies the American Revolution, I have the students do the wood stove problem to help them relate the advances of the past to their own living rooms in the present. Another POW that I do relating to heat during this time is about insulation. When the history teacher talks about the incidents at Valley Forge, the science class answers this question:

Many people died in Valley Forge by freezing to death. If you were in charge of issuing clothes to the men to keep warm, how would you tell them to dress? Assume that you just got a shipment of clothes and write a letter to the men describing how they should dress to keep the warmest. These soldiers aren't very likely to do what you say without an explanation . . . so be sure to use the information you have gained to explain the "why" to them.

Not only does this problem put students in a historical situation, it also forces them to think about the scientific reasons behind the way people dress, and how to teach these reasons to someone else. They will probably remember this POW next time they dress for the cold. There are some more sample questions, as well as student responses, at the end of this chapter.

These questions are incredibly effective in finding out what the students truly gained from the lessons and activities of the previous week. It gives true purpose to activities that we do in class.

The students like these too. One girl gave me great feedback on the POW in a discussion I had with her. She said, "I really like the POWs. They are a lot of work, but it's not like you have to cram for a test. I actually learn while I'm doing it." Students not only learn science while they are doing the POW, they also learn how to express themselves. On the following pages are some sample problems of the week as given to the students in my class. They are from a variety of scientific topics and require different styles of answers.

Mark Twain Earthquake

Read the firsthand description of an earthquake below. Then act as though you are the geologist that a newspaper has come to for an interview to explain the scientific reasons for what Mark Twain saw and felt. Write that explanation and include the causes of earthquakes, what type of plate movement is happening off the coast of San Francisco, P, S, and L waves, and the probable cause of the brick building falling apart.

It was just after noon, on a bright October day. I was coming down Third Street. The only objects in motion anywhere in sight in that thickly built and populous quarter were a man in a buggy behind me, and a streetcar wending slowly up the cross street. Otherwise, all was solitude and a Sabbath stillness.

As I turned the corner, around a frame house, there was a great rattle and jar, and it occurred to me that here was an item!—no doubt a fight in that house. Before I could turn and seek the door, there came a terrific shock; the ground seemed to roll under me in waves, interrupted by a violent joggling up and down, and there was a heavy grinding noise as of brick houses rubbing together. I fell up against the frame house and hurt my elbow. I knew what it was now . . . a third and still severer shock came, and as I reeled about on the pavement trying to keep my footing, I saw a sight! The entire front of a tall four-story brick building on Third Street sprung outward like a door and fell sprawling across the street, raising a great dust-like volume of smoke!

And here came the buggy—overboard went the man, and in less time than I can tell it the vehicle was distributed in small fragments along three hundred yards of street. . . . The streetcar had stopped, the horses were rearing and plunging, the passengers were pouring out at both ends, and one fat man had crashed halfway through a glass window on one side of the car, got wedged fast, and was squirming and screaming like an impaled madman. Every door, of every house, as far as the eye could reach, was vomiting a stream of human beings; and almost before one could execute a wink and begin another, there was a massed multitude of people stretching in endless procession down every street my position commanded.

Mark Twain

Figure 6.1. Science Problem of the Week #8.

Colonizing the Planets: Where Would You Go?

This week and last week we have studied lots of data about the planets. Are there any that would be suitable for humans to actually settle on in the future? Which would you go to? Why?

Write a paragraph explaining which planet you would colonize and why. Defend your choice by comparing at least three different parts of data on three different planets. For example, you may compare the temperatures, surface, and weather patterns; or the surface, composition of the atmosphere, and length of the day. Use whatever day helped you make the decision. (For comparison, earth's atmosphere is made of nitrogen, oxygen, carbon dioxide, and water vapor.)

Figure 6.2.   Science Problem of the Week #4.

Eruption vs. Revolution

Since we live near volcanoes, we need to pay close attention to the condition of the mountains around us, so we can tell if they are going to erupt. In science we have been studying the events that lead to an eruption. In history you've read and studied the events that lead up to the revolution. Are there any similarities between the events that lead to an eruption and the events that lead to revolution?

Describe in detail each of the three warning signs that come before an eruption. After each description, name at least two events that led up to the revolution, that would represent those warning signs before an eruption.

Remember that an excellent paper will have both an introduction and a conclusion.

Figure 6.3.   Science Problem of the Week #9.

Soil in the Expanding Nation

Wow! There a lot of connections between the subjects again these last few weeks. In science we have been studying soils and using math to calculate percentages of silt, sand, and clay. In Language Arts you are reading Animal Farm, which takes place on a farm. In history you learned that, during the time right after the Constitution was written, the colonies' main economy was farming and agriculture.

As you now know, many colonists eventually went west to establish homesteads in the new unsettled territory because the soil was great for farming. Before they could farm effectively, however, they needed to know some things about the soil. They didn't have the information necessary to make a good decision—you do!

Act as though you are a geologist working for the United States Department of Agriculture and respond to a letter from some of these early settlers in the area that you studied in history class. They have written to you to ask how they can determine if the soil on their land is good. Your letter back should inform them of the following things:

- The type of general soil order and a description of it. (Use the U.S. soils map.)

- How to find the type of soil texture.

- The four factors in determining what the soil is good for.

- What chemical elements should be present in the soil for it to be able to grow crops well.

- It should be in letter form. (Get creative: use Dear . . . and Sincerely . . .)

You are doing your country a great service by helping out these farmers. Thanks for a job well done!

To answer this question well you will need:

1. The questions from the text

2. The chart from when the guest speaker was here

3. The soil texture lab

4. U.S. soils map

Just keep getting better!

Figure 6.4. Science Problem of the Week #12.

Part 2
Evaluating the Problem of the Week

The Rubric

When grading writing, labs, and projects, I always struggled with the criteria that I used to score them, and worried about subjectivity. Although I had a vision and method of evaluation in my head, if asked to fully explain it, I felt a little pressed. As the students turned in their papers, they had no idea what grade they would receive. Rather than reinvent the wheel, I went searching for a better way of grading and found it in the language arts department. I "honorably adopted" the rubric, taking what had been used for years in language arts classes to evaluate writing, and adapting it to fit my science class.

A rubric is a point scale that the teacher, student, and parent can use to score a student's ability to show understanding of a subject, and his ability to communicate it. The rubric not only needs to be clear to the teacher as she is scoring work, but also to the students so they know how their work is being scored. Typically, a rubric's point scale starts at 0 and goes to 6. A score of 6 is for the very best papers. A score of 0 is for a paper that is never turned in at all.

There are two ways to develop a rubric. One way is to have the students construct their own grading scale, and the other is to have the teacher create it.

Student-generated rubrics work amazingly well because the students have "buy-in" to the evaluation process and thus internalize and respond better to their projects. It is no longer a mystery to them how a grade happens. They know. If students have never generated a rubric, or have never been given the chance to evaluate themselves, they need a lot of guidance.

This is how I generate a rubric with my class. First we discuss what is the most important part of an assignment. In a science class, the most important part is whether the answer is correct or not. Then we discuss smaller points such as completeness, grammar and spelling, and neatness, in order to further define the things that make papers poor, okay, good, or excellent. The discussions can be very eye-opening as the students struggle to determine what makes a great paper. I always find that the students create tougher criteria for a high score than I would. The benefit of this is that it puts all the power into the students' hands. The teacher's job is to compare their work to what they decided was good. Of course, a teacher needs to be careful to ensure that what they say is a good paper is truly good. There are always classes that will take this activity as a joke and not do it well. If that occurs, the teacher should develop the rubric himself.

Teacher-generated rubrics have no student input. This method allows the teacher to completely control the desired outcome. It can be put together with the help of the language arts teacher, who is familiar with grading writing in this way. The standard can be set to match the teacher's expectations. Remember, it is the student's job to strive toward the expectations, not the teacher's job to lower them. Make a 6 something for which students, even the usual A students, really have to work. If what is expected is clearly outlined in the rubric, students can truly decide their own grades.

In an effort to make the rubric easier to understand and follow, I again "honorably adopted" an idea, this time from geologists. One way that geologists classify rocks is with a dichotomous key. This gives the user two choices to help narrow down the possibilities of the type of rock. I put my rubric into this same format, emphasizing at each choice what was important to me. Grading simply becomes a process of following the flow of the quality factors. Not only can the teacher grade papers simply and effectively this way, but it also becomes easy for the students to understand and evaluate themselves.

Quality Factors and Operational Definitions

As the rubric begins to take shape, the delineations between the scores become apparent. Words such as "complete," "professional," and "superior" begin to emerge. These terms become the *quality factors* of a well-done assignment. The rubric key in Figure 6.5 shows each score and the quality factors that lead to them. A student who has achieved a score of 6 has a completely correct and complete answer that has superior support, no grammar or spelling errors, professional appearance and a visual that helps support and clarify the answer. That's quite an achievement! The following are the quality factors that are used in my class when evaluating a POW.

Correct

Complete

Professional appearance

Well-supported facts

Directions followed

Proper form (that is, a letter, a paragraph, or the assigned essay form)

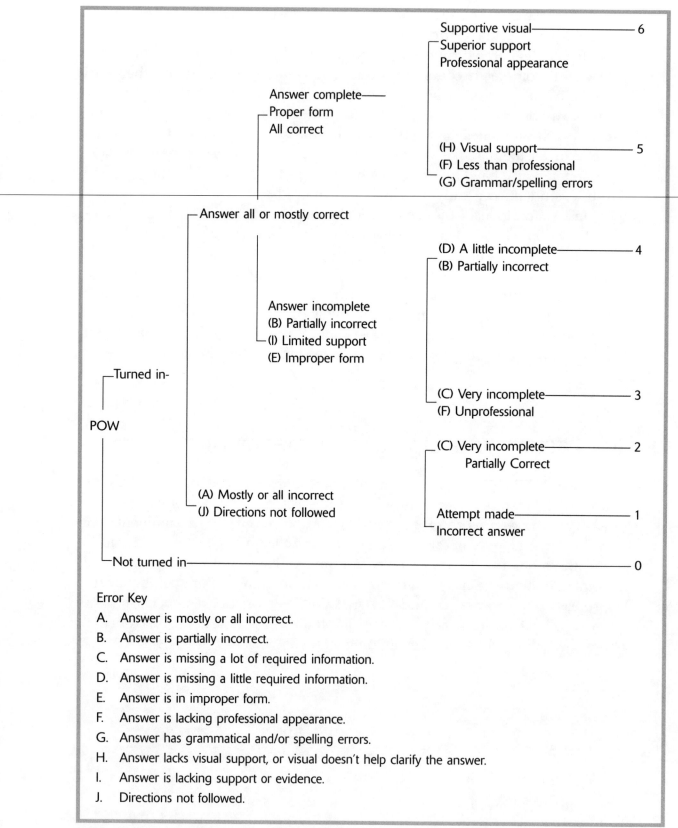

Figure 6.5. Problem of the Week rubric.

Correct grammar and spelling

A supportive visual that helps to clarify the answer

These quality factors are keyed by letter at the bottom of the rubric for clarification. The reasons for displaying the quality factors on the rubric will be explained and clarified in Part 3 of this chapter.

These quality factors can be developed by the teacher, or the students can help to generate them when writing the rubric. It is always ideal to have the students generate the quality factors, so that they feel a sense of ownership and understanding in the evaluation process. This can be done with the aid of two quality tools: the *Affinity Diagram* and the *Fishbone Diagram*.

Because of their prior school experiences, most students know what qualities an excellent paper or project possesses. Thus I ask them to generate these qualities. An Affinity Diagram is a method of brainstorming and organization that condenses ideas into major categories. At the beginning of the year, I give each student a small pile of Post-it notes and tell them to write down a different characteristic of a high-quality paper or project on each Post-It note. For example, a student may write "no spelling errors" on one note and "no smudges" on another. I give them about 10 minutes to brainstorm as many of these qualities as they can. Then, in groups of eight, I have them organize all the Post-it notes into similar categories. For example: "no wrinkles," "no smudges," "typed," "color," and "neatly written" could all go in the same category. The group then puts a name at the top of each category, such as "Appearance," so that it looks similar to Figure 6.6. The class can then combine each group's categories into a chart that includes everyone's ideas.

This group of ideas is then easily transferred into the Fishbone Diagram. The Fishbone Diagram is used to show cause and effect on a chart that looks remarkably like a fish without meat and scales. The effect is put into the head of the fish, and the causes are placed at the ends of each bone. If the desired effect in the class is high-quality work, that would be in the head of our fish.

Grammar	**Appearance**
Proper spelling	No wrinkles
Proper punctuation	No smudges
Complete sentences	Use color
	Typed
	Neatly written

Figure 6.6. Affinity Diagram for quality factors.

The categories that the students generated then become the causes and the labels for the bones (see Figure 6.7). The ideas that fill each of the categories become smaller bones and help to define each category.

The meaning of each category is called its *operational definition*. An *operational definition*, according to *Improvement Tools for Education (K–12)*, is "a clear, concise, and detailed definition of a measure" (1992). Once the Affinity and Fishbone Diagrams have been completed, its easy to take the ideas in each category and turn them into operational definitions. These then become the standards, generated by students, that all POWs are graded against. Nearly all subjectivity is removed from the grading, and evaluation becomes a comparison to a set standard. The Fishbone Diagram can then be put on chart paper and hung on the wall so that it can be referenced whenever clarification is needed.

As stated earlier, it is ideal if the students take part in the development of the quality factors. The high standards that the students set for themselves often pleasantly surprise me. However, there are also situations where the students are unable to handle the responsibility, or don't generate high enough standards. This is, of course, where the teacher's professional judgment comes in. If the students cannot be part of the process, then the teacher must generate the quality factors. There is definitely nothing wrong with this, as long as the operational definitions of the factors are clear to the students. This allows them to be clear on the areas that they will need to improve later.

Whatever the method of creating the rubric and quality factors, once completed, the rubric takes nearly all subjectivity out of the grading. The students are put in charge of their own grades, and the teacher is no longer a "bad

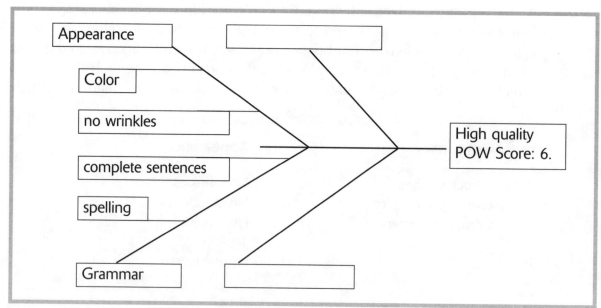

Figure 6.7. Fishbone Diagram for operational definitions.

guy" who gives grades but rather a "coach" who guides each student to overcome his or her particular weakness to meet the standard.

The students know that the rubric states clearly what is expected in their answers. However, they also need to be trained to grade themselves and others with the rubric. I train them by having the students grade random papers from the last year's students, with no names, so that they can see if their evaluations match my own. For the first year, the students can either be trained on their own papers, or the teacher can write some examples for them to use. (They also get training through the use of "The Progress Chart," discussed in the Part 3 of this chapter.) Properly trained students become very aware of what they will receive on their papers when they turn them in. This empowers the students because they can evaluate themselves and therefore be in real control of their grades.

One student was a very high achiever and was always driven to do her best. When presented with the Problems of the Week, she proceeded to answer the questions as she knew how, not according to the new high standard set by the rubric. After she got a 5 three weeks in a row, she came to me sure that I had made a mistake in her grade. She stated her case very well and I smiled. I simply asked her if she had looked at the quality factors and the operational definitions of what was required for a 6 by the rubric. She said "No, I've always gotten the highest grade with the way I write." Then she pulled out the rubric, compared it to the operational defintions on the wall, and found exactly what she was doing wrong. She never got another 5.

In order to get a 6, students will truly have to extend themselves. They will need to use all of the resources and information they have gathered in class to answer the question correctly, completely, neatly, and in proper writing form with no spelling or grammatical errors. They will also need to produce a visual that actually supports and helps explain the answer—not one that just looks pretty. This last piece, the visual, is where many of my students have a hard time. They are used to getting better grades when they use pretty or cute graphics. Graphics that are cute don't help to explain or clarify the answer. These students learn quickly how to use a visual to support their answers.

I give my students their POWs on a Friday and collect them on the following Friday. By giving the question to the students a week before it is due, I give them time to clarify the information that they gathered the week before. Some of the students will give me their POWs on Tuesday, so that I may read them and give them comments before they do their final drafts. Only one student who did this failed to receive a 5 or a 6 when he turned it in on Friday.

I also monitor and graph the turn-in percentages of these POWs. One year I notice a disturbing downward trend in the number of POWs that were turned in on time. In our class, negative trends are the students', not the teacher's, problem. It is the students' job to give me information that will help me change the system to correct the problem. So I gave the problem to them. I told them to let me know what I could change in the system to help reverse the trend. They gave me some great feedback. Many students indicated that I was giving them way too much time to forget. I then polled the class to find out how many of them needed all week to do the problem. Ninety percent did their POW on Thursday just before it was due. I asked, "If I gave it out on Thursday, would the percentages go up?" Most nodded yes. There were some, however, that really liked having time to get organized and let the question brew in their minds until Thursday. The solution that they finally arrived at was wonderful. They decided that if I made the POW available on Monday, those who wished to could get an early start. Then I would formally hand it out on Thursday to those who normally did it that night anyway. They said this would produce increase in turn-in percentages. They were right! The next week every class had a jump in its percentage, and they stayed higher the rest of the year! When given the chance, the students are more than capable of solving classroom system problems.

Whatever the particular method of creating a rubric, one thing is very important. It must be simple to understand—clear to both teachers and students. The students should have a copy of the rubric and the operational definitions with their 100 Facts List, or in their Continuous Improvement Journals. When the boys and girls know what is expected of them, they are more likely to strive for higher scores. It takes the mystery out of grading.

By the end of the year, those students that put in the time see a remarkable improvement in their ability to answer questions. They also find that they remember the information better. When they have to research their own notes to find the answers, and then write them in their own words, the knowledge stays with them. They learn to keep well-organized notes that are neat and easy to find.

The rubric is easy to use when grading the papers. It is not hard to get through 150 papers in an hour or two. As I mentioned, the first year I gave these POWs I only had 60 students. When I switched to a team with 150 students, I changed from giving the POWs weekly to giving them biweekly. This still allowed plenty of opportunities for evaluation, yet it didn't overload me or the students.

The workload can be modified by letting the students do the evaluating. If the students are trained to use the rubric well, they can score other students' papers very accurately. I find, as I'm sure all teachers have found, that students are usually harder on their own papers, and those of their peers, than the teacher is. I found that I let them evaluate each others' papers once in a while, the evaluations are just as effective as if I graded them all myself. If a student has a problem with the way another student scored his paper, the teacher can become the mediator and final judge. If the quality factors are well defined, however, this is rarely a problem.

The Problem of the Week has become a major component in the evaluation of my students. So much so that the POW and the Weekly Ten quizzes have eliminated the need for other testing. Everything is based on improving the students' learning over time, not on what the students know on a particular day. They know that, just like in life, bad days happen, mistakes can be corrected, and improvement can happen.

Unlike the weekly facts, these POWs are graded. At my school, like most others, we still give a letter grade at the end of each quarter and semester. Although different teachers do it different ways, the way that works best for me is a percentage based on the rubric score. For example: Each POW in my class is worth 40 points. So, if I use percentages and the rubric together, I give 100 percent for a 6, 92 percent for a 5, 85 percent for a 4, 75 percent for a 3, 65 percent for a 2, and 50 percent for a 1. The only way to get 0 percent is to not turn it in. Any late POWs are knocked down one rubric score. This method has kept everyone happy so far. I long for the day when these graphs, rather than letter grades will be their report cards.

Part 3
Tracking and Managing POW Improvement

Just as the Weekly Ten quiz is used to track growth and improvement in students' information, it is important to track growth and improvement in the students' ability to communicate and solve problems in their POWs. A student's score reflects not only what she knows, but also how well she can communicate it. The rubric is set up so that students who know the right answers but can't convey them well receive a 4, which loosely translates to a B. So the poor writer is not handicapped in her science grade. Also, the excellent writer who is used to great grades but doesn't follow the directions, or doesn't know the answer, receives a 2. I've had many beautifully written papers that didn't answer the question. The students who write them are very shocked that such a beautiful piece could receive a 2, but they have to display the correct knowledge! My role as the teacher, is to focus on bringing the 1s, 2s, and 3s into the 4 range. Students that can write a 4 can write a 5 or a 6 if they put a little more effort into answering the question fully. They can work with both the language arts teacher and the science teacher to help bring up their scores. Obviously the 2s and the 1s need the most help. Usually they just need to care. Those that accept help and put forth effort, however, see remarkable improvement.

Student progress and growth are tracked in two ways. Each student has his own special run chart, called the progress chart, so that he can see each week if there is growth. The entire class is also tracked on the Continuous Improvement Board (discussed in chapter 4) on a class run chart similar to that for the weekly facts.

Deming's Twelfth Point (adapted for the science classroom)

Students must be put in charge of their own continuous improvement and be motivated intrinsically so that they take pride in their accomplishments. Take away grading based on number of assignments turned in, and give the students criteria for high quality and help them to achieve it.

The Progress Chart

The progress chart is a special kind of run chart that helps students become more accurate evaluators of their own work. According to Deming's profound knowledge theory, learning cannot be based on experience alone. It requires comparisons of results to a predicted plan or theory. He indicates that predicting why something happens is essential to understanding results and continually improving (Deming 1986).

Most students don't understand why or how their grades are determined. This is especially true with projects and writing assignments. To help combat this and help the students understand, I have them keep track on a progress chart (see Figure 6.8) for each POW. (This type of chart was originally created and used by Jim Genty, a teacher at Leander High School in Texas. I changed it a little to better suit my purposes and this application.) When students turn in their POWs, I have them evaluate themselves based on the quality factors in the rubric. They draw a circle in the box that indicates the score they *predict* they will get. When they get their answers back,

POW Progress Chart

Key – O = Predicted score   X = Actual score   R = Rewrite score

For:

POW #	1	2	3	4	5	6	7	8	9	10	11	12	13	14	15	16	17	18	19
Score																			
6																			
5																			
4																			
3																			
2																			
1																			
Didn't do																			
Late																			

Figure 6.8. Blank student progress chart for POW.

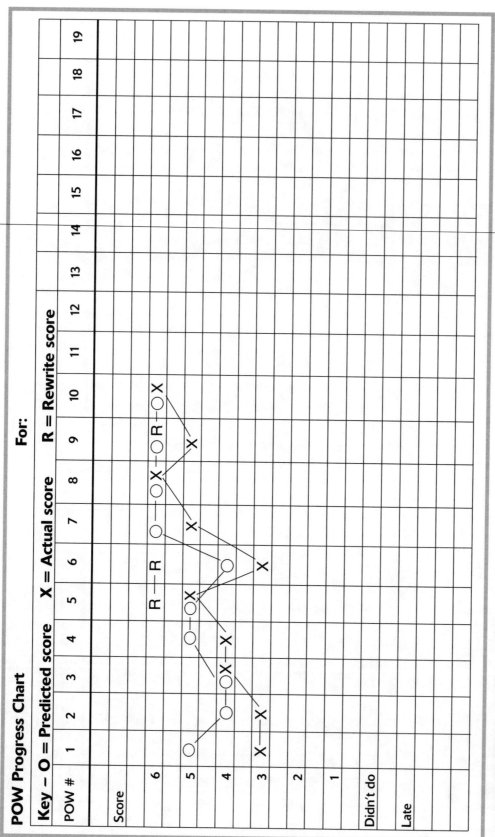

Figure 6.9. Sample student progress chart.

they put an "X" for their actual score. It's not surprising that many students predict higher grades than they actually achieve the first few times. In time, however, as they grow used to the quality factors and their operational definitions, they become very good at the evaluations.

There is also a third mark that goes on the graph. If they chose to rewrite their POW, they put an "R" on the *rewrite* score. This is a good indication of whether they are beginning to understand what is needed to answer the question effectively. If a student can rewrite his paper and achieve a 6, he usually begins to get 6s on the first try soon there after. (See Figure 6.9.)

The Error Chart

In order for the students to do the rewrite, they need to know where to improve. To help focus their improvement, the students are told which of the quality factors they failed to meet. Often in my own school career, I received a score on a paper or a project without really knowing why. My teacher said it was a C, and I learned not to question the authority. Worse yet, many times in my teaching career I have given a score because I felt that the paper deserved it, yet if I were really pressed, I don't think I could have given concrete reasons. The rubric, in unison with the quality factors, eliminates most of the subjectiveness in the grading by specifying what is expected. The Error Chart helps the students see exactly what needs to be improved. (See Figure 6.10.)

At the bottom of the rubric (Figure 6.5) there are 10 quality factors students may fail to meet. By listing them on the paper the students have, and also on the one the teacher uses to correct, all is made clear. When scoring the paper, the teacher follows the rubric and makes notations about which quality factors the student fails to meet. If there are grammatical or punctuation errors, a "g" is put at the top of the student's paper. If part of the required information is missing, a "d" goes next to the "g." With those two errors, the student's score would be a 4.

The students then take this information and plot it on their *error charts* (Figure 6.11) in their continuous improvement journals. The error chart is designed so they simply shade the box next to each error they make. Each POW is plotted in this same way. As the year progresses, the students begin to see definite patterns in the way that they answer questions. They see that they aren't being careful to answer the whole question, that they need to proofread for grammar and spelling, or that they need to work on getting the whole answer correct. Each student will make their own errors, and the error chart will give them the information they need to make the right

POW Error Chart   **For:**

Shade the box next to each error made.

POW #	1	2	3	4	5	6	7	8	9	10	11	12	13	14	15	16	17	18	19
Possible errors																			
All or most incorrect (a)																			
A little incorrect (b)																			
A lot missing (c)																			
A little missing (d)																			
Improper form (e)																			
Not professional (f)																			
Grammar and spelling (g)																			
Visual support problem (h)																			
Incomplete support (i)																			
Follow directions (j)																			

Figure 6.10. Blank student error chart.

POW Error Chart

For:

Shade the box next to each error made.

POW #	1	2	3	4	5	6	7	8	9	10	11	12	13	14	15	16	17	18	19
Possible errors																			
All or most incorrect (a)																			
A little incorrect (b)	■																		
A lot missing (c)	■	■				■													
A little missing (d)			■	■															
Improper form (e)	■																		
Not professional (f)	■	■																	
Grammar and spelling (g)	■	■						■	■										
Visual support problem (h)	■																		
Incomplete support (i)																			
Follow directions (j)																			

Figure 6.11. Sample student error chart.

improvements. An individual education plan is established without formally sitting down and creating an individual plan! This is a powerful tool in training the students to answer questions better in general. Their goal is to eliminate the errors. They want to stop having to shade anything!

I share with my students the Alcoholics Anonymous definition of insanity: "Doing the same thing over and over and expecting a different result." The goal, of course, is to stop making the same mistakes. When they have the types of mistakes they are making right in front of them, it is easy to see how to improve.

The first week I ever used the error chart, a student who got a 4 came in the very next day with his POW rewritten. When I scored it, it was clearly a 6. I asked him right then why he rewrote it. He said that for the first time he knew exactly what he had done wrong, and since he knew he could fix it, he did.

While I'm correcting the papers, I also keep track of the errors that the whole class is making. I use the same chart, only this time I shade the proper box each time a mistake is made by anyone in the class. When I'm done, I have a beautiful histogram showing the quality factors that need the most improving in each class. (See Figure 6.12.) By doing this I can tailor my presentation of the POW to each class when it is handed out the next week. I show them the histogram and emphasize being careful on the most common errors.

The results speak for themselves. In the three weeks following the first implementation of the error chart, the number of 6s increased from two the first week to nine the second week and nineteen the third week. The students got excited. The number of rewrites went way up and the focus each week really turned to improving.

The growth can be seen in the class charts. It was after POW #9 that the students began to use the error chart. Figure 6.13 shows a run chart that represents a lot of improvement past POW #10. Figure 6.14 shows the totals for the class up to POW #8. Figure 6.15 shows the class totals from POW #9, to the last POW, which was number 15. Notice the definite shift to the right in the students' scores.

When the same errors are being repeated over and over by a class, I ask them to tell me how I can change the system to help them reduce those types of errors. Once a class was struggling and continually giving answers that were partially incomplete. It seemed that they knew all the information but weren't reading the questions carefully. I asked them what I could do to help. One student said, "In our history class we have learned how to take notes in 'bullet form.' Is there any way you could list all the things that we have to answer in bullet form so that we could check them off as we go?"

I did, and that kind of error decreased!

POW Error Chart

For:

Shade the box next to each error made.

POW #	1	2	3	4	5	6	7	8	9	10	11	12	13	14	15	16	17	18	19
Possible errors																			
All or most incorrect (a)	▮	▮																	
A little incorrect (b)	▮	▮	▮	▮															
A lot missing (c)	▮	▮	▮	▮	▮														
A little missing (d)	▮	▮	▮	▮	▮	▮	▮	▮	▮	▮	▮								
Improper form (e)	▮	▮																	
Not professional (f)	▮	▮	▮	▮	▮														
Grammar and spelling (g)	▮	▮	▮	▮	▮	▮													
Visual support problem (h)	▮	▮	▮	▮	▮	▮	▮	▮	▮										
Incomplete support (i)	▮	▮																	
Follow directions (j)	▮	▮																	

Figure 6.12. Sample class error chart.

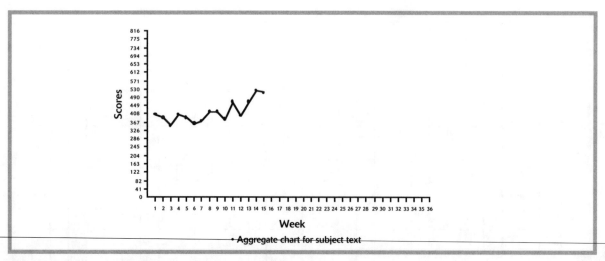

Figure 6.13. Problem of the Week run chart.

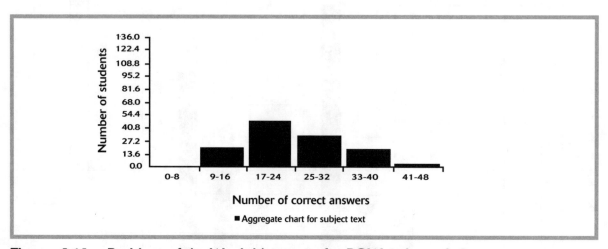

Figure 6.14. Problem of the Week histogram for POW 1 through 8.

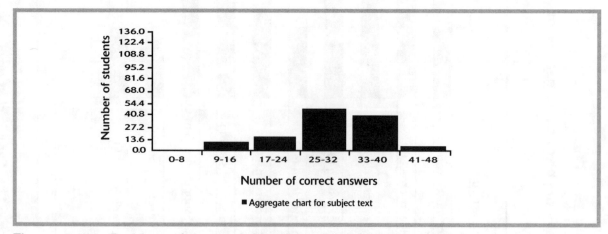

Figure 6.15. Problem of the week histogram for POW 8 through 15.

The rubric, quality factors, and error chart, in conjunction with the progress chart, provide clear concrete feedback to the students on exactly what is expected and what needs to change before they can receive higher scores. Not only does it take the emphasis off the score and put in on improving, it becomes an individualized education for each student, as they try to correct the errors that they continually make.

Rewrites

Since my emphasis is on helping the student to improve, I let the students do rewrites if they feel that they can do a better job. I always let the desire to improve be student driven. If students want to make corrections and do a rewrite for a better grade they can. The new score does not change the class graph. The work they put in will affect their grades, though, and what they learn in the rewrite will show up in better answers to future POWs. The key here is that the student is redoing the assignment for *his* reasons.

One student I'll call Ricky is a great example. Ricky was satisfied with 1s and 2s on his POWs until his mom saw his grade. He came to me desperate at the end of the quarter, and asked how he could bring up his grade. He was hoping to get some book work or a ditto. I don't believe in busy work for extra credit, so I told him that the only way was to redo his POWs for higher scores. He needed to prove he knew the information. He walked out a little disappointed, but knew he had to prove what he knew in order for his grade to improve. He went back through his old materials and notes and turned in five redone POWs. With a little help, encouragement, and the knowledge of how to use the rubric and error chart, the extra effort and study paid off with four 5s and a 6. His grade went up because he showed he knew the material.

Some students don't convey their knowledge well on paper. This is a marvelous chance to sit with them in small groups and help them get better at answering questions. I hold clinics after school once every other week for those scoring low consistently. With the error chart, it is easy to see what they need help with. If the science teacher can work well with the language arts teacher, they can also help the students with the papers. Maybe they can even be used as a grade in both classes! Language arts courses can now serve another purpose, beyond reading great literature and writing papers for the English class. They can teach students how to express themselves when answering questions in other subject areas. Wow! I wish I had been more prepared for all the blue book essay tests that I took in college. With the personal attention at these clinics, students always begin to improve. Not only do their own graphs look better, but they help the class graph to improve.

Key Points

- Knowledge cannot be evaluated using a multiple-choice test.

- Students need opportunities to apply or reteach what they know.

- Problems of the Week are developed around the idea of putting students in realistic situations and letting them use the information they have learned to explain or solve a problem.

- Knowledge should be judged as a gymnast is judged in competition, by a set of quality factors with clear operational definitions. This takes nearly all subjectivity out of the grading process.

- One way to do this is through a rubric.

- Students can take charge of their own improvement by keeping track of the quality factors that they need to work on and striving to improve in those areas.

- Students' grades can be increased only by rewriting their Problems of the Week to show they know the material.

- Students keep track of their own improvement. Teachers keep track of class improvement and tailor their classes to emphasize the types of quality factors each class needs to improve.

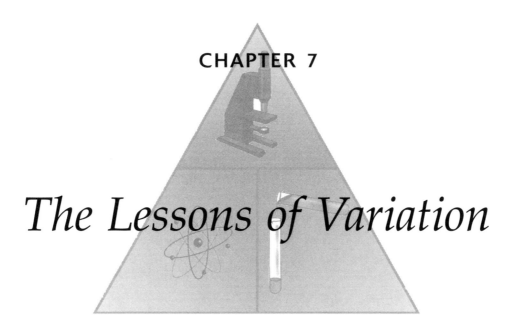

CHAPTER 7

The Lessons of Variation

There will be improvement. It can't help but happen. Yet there is also variation. This variation can seem very frustrating to the students at first. The ups and downs each week can cause a roller coaster of emotions that detract from the central purpose. If variation is handled properly, however, the students come to expect it and learn from it. The two types of variation that the students need to become aware of are Common Cause Variation and Special Cause Variation.

Common Cause Variation

The students are constantly being evaluated. Once a week they are evaluated on their Weekly Ten. Biweekly they are evaluated on the Problem of the Week. They are evaluated on their projects, and they are evaluated by the substitutes that come in. Because the evaluations are done on charts, the students see the graphs going up and down each week. At first, the students think that if they don't improve every week, it's bad.

They especially feel this with their own personal run charts. Near the beginning of the year, with each Weekly Ten I have to be ready either to celebrate the continued growth, or to talk to them about variation. It's necessary to show them that on any given day the dice may roll several questions that they know, or several that they do not. When the graph goes down I simply say, "That's okay, it was a tough bunch of questions. We'll do better next time." After I say this a few times, the students pick up on the positive tone and begin to say it themselves. I bring in examples of stock market reports with growth graphs to show them how up-and-down stocks are. The students learn that smart people don't look at the small ups and downs; they look at the general trends. Is there overall growth over time? That's what matters!

After four or five weeks of up-and-down scores, students will actually begin to say, "Wow, that was a tough bunch of questions. I need to study that section more." Or, "That's okay. We'll do better next time." This is a lot different from what they say at the beginning of the year, which is more like "We're dumb!"

Variation comes and goes with the class scores as well. After the first quarter, the large variations come from student absences, as the cold and flu season sets in. This bothered the class at first. Their individual scores were going up, but it seemed as though the class scores were not keeping pace. A student suggested that along with the class total we also do a class average. This was a great suggestion, since even if the class total went down they could see that individual scores were still going up.

I keep track of several things in the classroom. We track substitute evaluation, work turn-in, enthusiasm, learning, Problem of the Week scores, and other factors. Variation occurs in all of these settings. It is also important for me as a teacher to understand common variation, and not think that I have to redo my program if something out of the ordinary happens.

Special Cause Variation

Sometimes things outside the classroom will come up that affect students' scores. A perfect example happened after my class had nearly steady growth for many weeks in a row. There were some small, common cause variations, but over all there was significant improvement. Then one week there was a big drop. The students were really upset, but I didn't make a big deal of it. I thought that maybe it was just a tough bunch of questions. The next week the scores shot back up and way past their previous score. I took a moment to ask the students what had happened the previous week. Without hesitation the students remarked that they had been completely focused on a project that was due in their language arts class. Many had stayed up all night to finish. I had completely forgotten about that assignment. That was a cause outside of the normal variation—a special cause! It was a wonderful teaching and learning moment. As teachers, we sometimes think that ours is the only class that students have in the day. Many times the students have to prioritize their time to meet the most urgent need, and that takes away from our classes. The students learn that even special cause variation is okay, as long as they don't stay focused on that low point. They can always rise again.

If the class wasn't structured toward improvement, that could have been a normal quiz, and everybody would have "bombed." But, by keeping improvement as the goal, it was okay that they had an off day. They could prioritize their time to get what was important done, and knew that they could bounce back the next week.

Another week, there were many students absent because of a school-related trip. The ones that remained didn't want to see the graph drop and begged that we skip the Weekly Ten that week. I explained to them that in a real world situation, there may be times when people can't or won't do their parts. It is then that the people who can step up their own performances and go for personal bests to compensate. The overall score of the class did take a big drop. Yet, even with 10 students missing, the class scored 20 points higher than it had five weeks earlier when everyone was there. There were many boys and girls who got their first 10s, and many others achieved their personal bests.

Extremely high scores can also be a source of special cause variation. One week, by luck of the dice, all the weekly fact questions for one class came from units that we had already done. This created an incredibly inflated score. They shot from a class total of 195 up to a 249. This special cause was pointed out and the numbers went back down the next week.

By teaching the students the differences in variation, the students can become better at analyzing lab results and observations. They begin to think critically about the results that they get and therefore draw better conclusions. They can become more adept at using data to make decisions.

Key Points

- When students begin to track and chart data, they will notice variation.
- This provides a wonderful opportunity to teach them about the causes of variation.
- With students, I focus on common and special causes of variation.
- Students learn to look for trends in data rather than focusing on isolated events.
- Students can learn to make good decisions based on data.

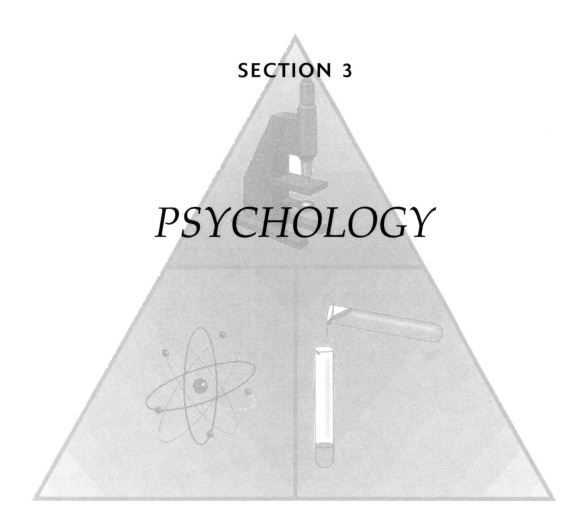

SECTION 3

PSYCHOLOGY

Improving student enthusiasm, behavior, and performance.

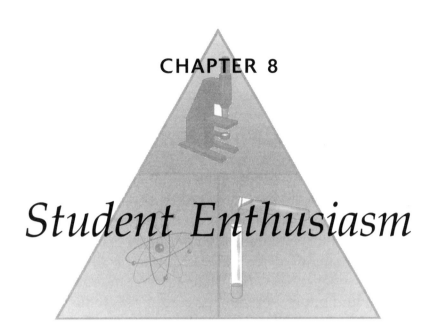

CHAPTER 8

Student Enthusiasm

Part 1
Monitoring Enthusiasm

One challenge to educators is maintaining students' enthusiasm. Children start life with an incredible desire to learn. Toddlers will strive to crawl and then to walk, falling down and getting back up over and over again until they master it. When five-year-olds start kindergarten, they still have that incredible desire to learn. As they go through our educational system, however, that desire is somehow not only lost, but sometimes absolutely crushed. When 11- and 12-year-olds get to junior high, dissatisfaction with the system and lack of desire to learn combine with their rebellious tendencies and turn into angry and resentful attitudes. The result is the common and incredible increase in behavior problems. An eighth-grade student summed it up perfectly in a moment of blatant honesty when he asked, "Why do we have to come and sit in a place we don't want to be, work with people we don't like to work with, to learn things that we don't want to learn?" This statement came from a brilliant young person who was an incredible behavior challenge. He knew full well that he was a disruption. He didn't see a reason to stop, and didn't see a reason to learn.

Science Life History

Where Have They Been?

One of the keys to understanding the decline in enthusiasm is to remember that as boys and girls mature they may not think as adults think, but they feel the same as adults feel, especially when treated unfairly, or abused mentally or emotionally. As a junior high teacher, I get a mixed bag of enthusiasm at the beginning of the year. Experiences that students have had previously in school are as varied as their faces. In order for me to do a good job, I need to find out where they have been, where they are now, and why they feel the way they do. Unfortunately, junior high students normally don't walk up to the teacher and say how they feel about their school lives. We usually find out through their behaviors in the classroom. However, there is a more effective and nonthreatening way to learn.

I use what I call the "Science Life History." This is a simple graph that lets students tell about their feelings through their previous years of school. The graph that I use is presented in Figure 8.1. Students place dots on their graphs that correspond to their feelings about science each year that they have been in school. Most young people remember feelings more than information, and students usually remember how they felt. If they don't remember, then obviously it made no impression at all, so I have them mark the "It was okay" line.

I give these graphs to the students during the first week of school. That gives me an idea right away of how they feel about science. The students have a chance to express their feelings in a nonconfrontational way on the paper. When I circulate around the room and watch their graphs, I get a good look at where the students are now, and where they came from. Not only does the graph give me a chance to get to know each of them individually, it also lets them know on the first day of school that I care about how they are feeling.

The data collected in these graphs can also be very helpful to the previous year's teacher. If the teachers are working together, as recommended in chapter 2, they need to know how the students view their experiences from the previous year. This is valuable especially because the student has had some time for reflection, which can lend more objectivity to his or her response.

Students generally get very introspective as they fill out the graphs. To take advantage of that contemplative time, I have them explain at the bottom of the graph sheet the reasons for their responses at each grade level. When the graphs are completed, it is amazing how revealing they are to the students and to the teacher. I then hold a discussion and keep track of the reasons for their highest peaks and their lowest valleys. The more students are asked to

Loved it!	
Liked it.	
OK, I guess.	
Didn't like it.	
Hated it!	
	Kindergarten First Second Third Fourth Fifth Sixth Seventh

Reasons

Kindergarten:_____

_____

First:_____

_____

Second:_____

_____

Third:_____

_____

Fourth:_____

_____

Fifth:_____

_____

Sixth:_____

_____

Seventh:_____

_____

Figure 8.1. Science Life History enthusiasm and learning graph.

Loved it!	
Liked it.	
OK, I guess.	
Didn't like it.	
Hated it!	
	Elementary Junior High High School College Graduate

Reasons

Elementary: _____
_____
_____

Junior High: _____
_____
_____

High School: _____
_____
_____

College: _____
_____
_____

Graduate: _____
_____
_____

Figure 8.2. Academic enthusiasm graph.

share, the more students want to share, and the more apparent it becomes that their feelings about a subject are shared by others. The most important thing I discovered is that their feelings very rarely relate to the *subject*. Rather, their feelings relate to what was going on in their lives at the time—moves, divorces, or trouble with friends. Often it is a reflection of the relationship with the teacher. Teachers know that no matter how hard they try to reach some students, they will still be disliked. Sometimes there is a personality conflict; other times it is the way the class is organized and operated. The actual *subject* rarely has anything to do with the students' feelings about it.

To understand the significance of feelings, readers can fill out the graph that follows in Figure 8.2. It is a little different from the graph I give the students, because teachers probably don't remember first-grade science. But they probably do recall how they *felt* about science in elementary school. It is important to fill out the bottom of the page to explain the reasons behind the placement of the dots. Filling out this sheet requires some thought and contemplation.

Science Life History in the Making

Where Are They Now?

After studying and learning from the science life history graphs, I give each student two more graphs that will reveal his reactions to his current eighth-grade experience. One of the graphs helps me to track the students' enthusiasm through the year. (Figure 8.3.) The other graph tracks how much they feel they are learning (Figure 8.4).

The students have copies of the learning graph and the enthusiasm graph in their continuous improvement journals (described in chapter 4). Once a month, I ask them to mark how they feel about the class on the enthusiasm graph, and whether they think they are learning on the learning graph.

First, they fill out their enthusiasm graphs by putting dots to show how they are feeling about the class today. Then, on the lines at the bottom, they write down the reasons for their placement of the dots. The "reason" section is there purely to help the students clarify their thinking. Then they put dots on their learning graphs to show whether they think they are learning. Many times, the students haven't realized that there is a difference. As we found on the science life histories, they often associate the teacher and the method with the subject; they almost always associate the learning with the liking.

ENTHUSIASM

Loved it!	
Liked it.	
OK, I guess.	
Didn't like it.	
Hated it!	
	September October November December January February March April May June

Reasons

September: _____

_____

October: _____

_____

November: _____

_____

December: _____

_____

January: _____

_____

February: _____

_____

March: _____

_____

April: _____

_____

May: _____

_____

Figure 8.3. Enthusiasm in the making graph.

LEARNING

	September October November December January February March April May June
Learned a lot!	
Learned quite a bit.	
Learned some.	
Didn't learn much.	
Learned nothing.	

Reasons

September: _____
_____

October: _____
_____

November: _____
_____

December: _____
_____

January: _____
_____

February: _____
_____

March: _____
_____

April: _____
_____

May: _____
_____

Figure 8.4.   Learning in the making graph.

These graphs help them to distinguish between the two. Some students, especially gifted children, can be very happy in a class yet know that they haven't learned anything. The students that hate school may realize that they are learning a lot, and that will be reflected in their graphs. The whole spectrum is usually represented. I make no judgments about their responses and I do not collect their graphs. The students, therefore, are free to respond honestly.

The students *are* very honest. This feedback has become a cornerstone for improvement in my classroom. If most members of the class do not feel as though they are learning, then I need to revise my curriculum. If most students do not like the class, I'd better find out why and change things.

To get an idea of how the whole class feels without reading each of their graphs, the students fill out a class summary graph. This graph is a combination of the learning and enthusiasm graphs that the students filled out for themselves (Figure 8.5). The horizontal axis shows the way they are feeling (enthusiasm), and the vertical axis shows how much they think that they have learned. This graph can be done either on poster paper or a transparency. If I use poster paper, which I did when I first started this, I give each student a large sticky dot that can be purchased at most office supply places. Each member of the class comes up individually, while the rest are doing some sort of seatwork, and puts his/her dot on the graph where his/her two graphs would meet. The finished class graph gives a great indication of how the class feels that day. (See Figure 8.6.)

When done on the overhead transparency, the process is still the same. I use smaller sticky dots and leave the overhead off until all of the dots are on the clear sheet. I teach five classes a day and the feedback from each class is valuable. Each class does its own graph, using the same representative colors as the class information run charts. I post each class graph on the Improvement Board (described in chapter 4). If I want an idea of how all of the classes together are feeling, I can simply lay one transparency over the other. (See Figure 8.7.)

My goal as the teacher is to get all of the dots high and to the right on the graph. That would mean that the students all like the class and feel as though they are learning. The students know that I don't know who puts the dots where, so I expect some jokers. For the most part, the students are very honest.

Because the students are honest, it's important not to take these responses lightly. Yet junior high students feel differently everyday. A student, asked the same question on two different days, could give two very different answers. I've had students that I know like the class and are learning, mark just the class graph, because they were unhappy with me that day. The chart, therefore, should be used to look for general trends, not individual ones. Is the graph moving up and to the right? Is the teacher maintaining a high level of enthusiasm and learning? Am I listening and responding to the students as my customers?

ENTHUSIASM VS. LEARNING

	Hated it!	Didn't like it.	OK, I guess.	Liked it.	Loved it!
Learned a lot!					
Learned quite a bit.					
Learned some.					
Didn't learn much.					
Learned nothing.					

Figure 8.5. Enthusiasm vs. learning graph.

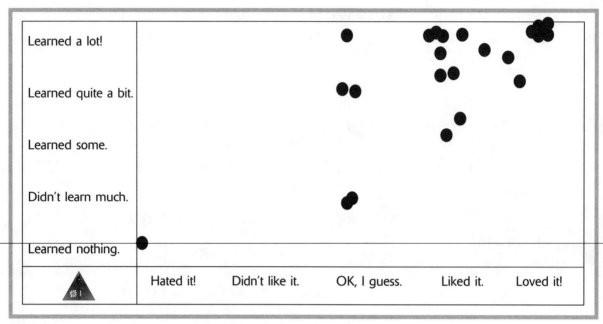

Figure 8.6. Single class enthusiasm vs. learning sample.

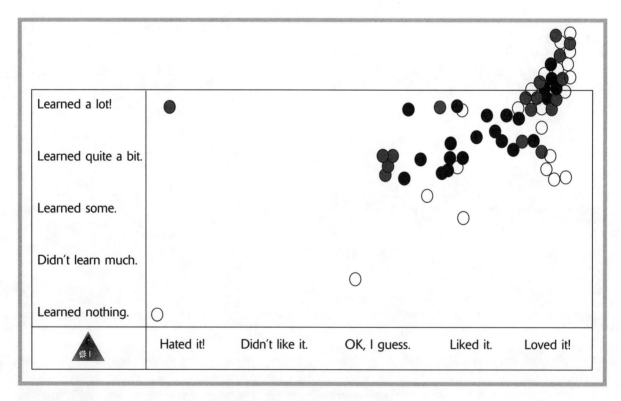

Figure 8.7. Entire team enthusiasm vs. learning sample.

Part 2
Improving Student Enthusiasm

"A teacher's job is not to motivate students, but rather find out what takes away their motivation, and stop doing it."

W. EDWARDS DEMING

Plus Delta Charts

Deming's Fourteenth Point (adapted for the science classroom)

Collect and take in feedback from parents, administrators, and students to make them part of the process of designing the best science program imaginable.

Now that the teacher has an impression of how the students perceive the class, there needs to be a method for obtaining specific information to make needed changes. Feedback is that method.

"Students have all the information necessary to make the classroom great, but none of the power. Teachers have all of the power and very little information."

L. JENKINS

The best way that I have found to get feedback is through a *Plus Delta chart.* (see Figure 8.8). This is a simple piece of paper with two columns. One side is the Plus side, where students list what they liked in the class that month. The other side is the Delta side. This is where students write the things they think need to change. The students fill out these charts once a month while doing their enthusiasm and learning graphs. I give them the opportunity not only to evaluate the class, but also to evaluate me. This can be very nerve

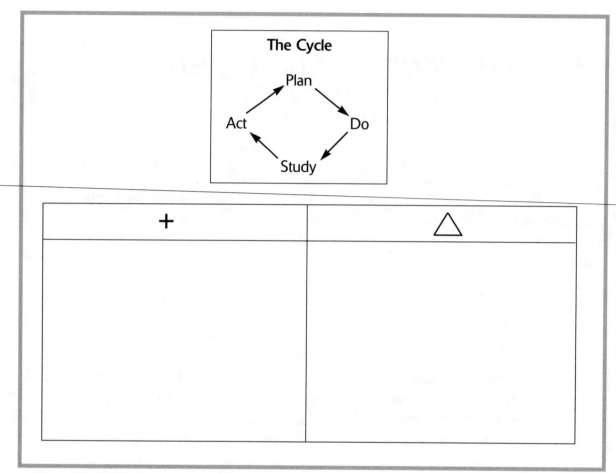

Figure 8.8. Plus Delta chart for the classroom.

wracking, yet if teachers are evaluating their students, it is important that students have the opportunity to evaluate their teachers.

Once the charts are filled out and the students have graded me, I take the papers home or have an aide tally the results. I make a list of the things that I did well and pat myself on the back. Then I list the things that the students say that I should change. Remember to keep in mind that children don't think as adults. There will be responses such as "Don't give us as much work," and so on. The comments are not always what I want to hear. There are months when I don't want to know what they think of my teaching. Yet, if we teachers truly want to grow and get better, we need to be able to take criticism from our customers. They are the ones who truly know. Whenever I didn't want to find out what the students really thought of my teaching, it was a sure indication that I knew I could have done better.

This is also a valuable way to get feedback from the parents. Teachers have to acknowledge that the parents are customers as well. If there is to be a customer focus, parents need to be included in the loop. In the course of the year, there are often only two positive contacts with the parents: Back-to-School Night and Open House. These are wonderful times to chitchat with parents, but not the proper time for criticism on any level. It is much better to get parent feedback consistently throughout the year. I send the Plus Delta charts home for the parents to fill out once per quarter (Figure 8.9). It can be done as often as is practical. The parents fill them out based on their perceptions and send them back with the students. I collect the information and respond much the same as I do with the students, only in a letter. This gives the teacher valuable feedback into what the parents think about the program, and about what the kids are saying. After all, the parents only get their information from

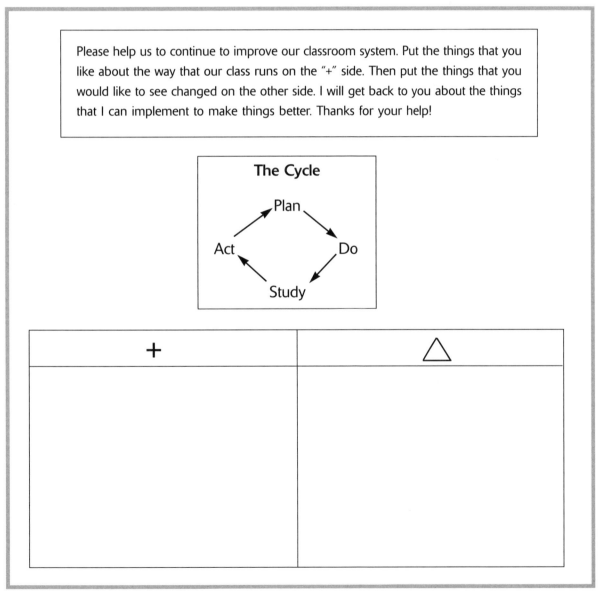

Figure 8.9. Parent Plus Delta chart.

the students. Sometimes parents' responses indicate that their children never talk to them about what goes on at school.

Invariably, the first time I send out the Parent Plus Delta chart, many students will come to me and say "How can my parents fill this out? They have no idea what I do here." I simply respond, "What a wonderful opportunity this is to get together and talk with them about it."

These Plus Delta graphs become "mini surveys." They are a vital source of contact and give the parents a forum from which to be heard. Often parents are frustrated because they feel powerless. With this forum, parents can play an active part in their child's education from a distance.

Teachers need to be prepared. If you don't want the feedback, don't ask the questions. The feedback from parents is incredible. They don't pull any punches. They will write things on that piece of paper that they might not say to a teacher directly. This is both good and bad. Teachers get some of the most honest compliments in the world, and some wonderful insights into how their programs and personalities affect their students' lives. Parents really appreciate positive influences and love to tell about it. They also will tell teachers where they can improve. Even though this may not always be easy to hear, it is important that teachers hear it.

There have been times in this process when I thought that the way I did things was having a wonderful effect on the students. The parents, however, saw frustrations and anger in the children at home, and they told me about it. Once a teacher hears criticism, he has three choices: ignore it, deny it, or change to get better. If you do either of the first two, you will never get an honest response again. Only give these Plus Delta graphs out if you have a true desire to improve.

Once teachers know what needs to change, there has to be a process through which change can be planned and executed.

The PDSA Cycle

Deming's Seventh, Tenth, and Fourteenth Points (adapted for the science classroom)

The purpose of the teacher is to help the students improve in all that they do and achieve all that they can achieve. This is done by removing the barriers within the classroom system that hinder enthusiasm and learning.

Once the information for making the changes has been obtained, the students can be shown, in a new context, the true power of the scientific method. Not all the students' suggestions are beneficial to themselves or the class. Deming said that theory, not experience, is the best teacher. Science teachers know that scientists have learned all that they know by hypothesizing and experimenting. If one way didn't work, the scientist tried another. Life is like that, but students very rarely see this example modeled. They see a lot of failure or success, but they rarely see the process through which success is obtained, or through which failure can be overcome, learned from, and no longer perceived as negative. This is a perfect opportunity to use the *PDSA Cycle*.

PDSA is an acronym that stands for *plan, do, study, act*. It is the scientific method in a different application, borrowed from the management tools of TQM. Once the feedback for improvement has been gathered, it's time to make a *plan* to put it into action. Then the teacher and students need to *do* the plan—actually implement what they decided to do. Then, *study* the results. Did it accomplish its objective? Once the analysis is done, *act* on that analysis by either continuing the process if it worked, or making a new plan and beginning the process all over again. This process is a spiral of constant improvement. Let me give you some examples of how I have used it.

One month, when discussing the Plus Delta charts, a problem emerged. The students were growing frustrated with the way I assigned homework. They didn't really object to the homework itself; they were frustrated with *how* it was assigned. This was a group of students that was very active extracurricularly. At the end of the period each day I would tell them what they had to do that evening. Sometimes it was a lot of work, sometimes it was a little. By coincidence, the previous few weeks, I had assigned the most homework on the nights when the boys and girls had the most things going on in their lives outside the class. "Oh yeah," I thought, "they do have things in their lives besides my class." I asked them to help find a solution.

Plan

After the discussion, they requested that I tell them on Monday the work that was assigned for the entire week. They could prioritize and get the work done when they wanted, as long as it was before Friday. I agreed to give it a try.

Do

I gave them the work for the week on Monday with a list of the day each assignment should be done. That way students who wanted to do the assignment the night it was actually assigned could. It would always be most beneficial to do it on the assigned night, but this format allowed those students who had big events during the week an opportunity to plan around them.

Study

Two wonderful things happened as a result. The students immediately became more relaxed, and some of the students even attempted to understand, on their own, what we would cover a few days later. There was suddenly an air of expectancy from those who were trying to work ahead. They came in knowing what they wanted to learn so that they could go on. The students noticed right away that it would always be most beneficial to do the work on the assigned night, but they really appreciated the freedom to do it when they had the time.

Act

This system worked exceptionally well, and we used it for the rest of the year. There were a few more minor modifications that were suggested and then dropped because they were ineffective in the study stage.

Piaget, the prominent child psychologist, revealed that children don't think as adults think, though they feel as adults feel. Just because the students or parents suggest something doesn't mean that the teacher should do it. The teacher is the trained professional in the room. The students don't always know what is good for them. Judgment and discernment need to be exercised when reading through or discussing the suggestions. In time, the students begin to understand which of their suggestions are not appropriate or impossible to implement. When the teacher talks with the students about their suggestions and explains why some will be considered and some won't, inappropriate suggestions slowly fade away. Remember that we are looking at improvement in all areas—improving the suggestions for improvement is one of these areas.

Over time, when the students work through the PDSA cycle, and teachers make the improvements necessary to remove the barriers that hinder enthusiasm, the class's monthly enthusiasm and learning graph begins to change. More and more students begin responding in ways that show they like the class and are learning. The example in Figure 8.10 shows three months of change the first year I implemented the PDSA cycle. As you can see, there was lots of room for improvement the first month. With the students' help,

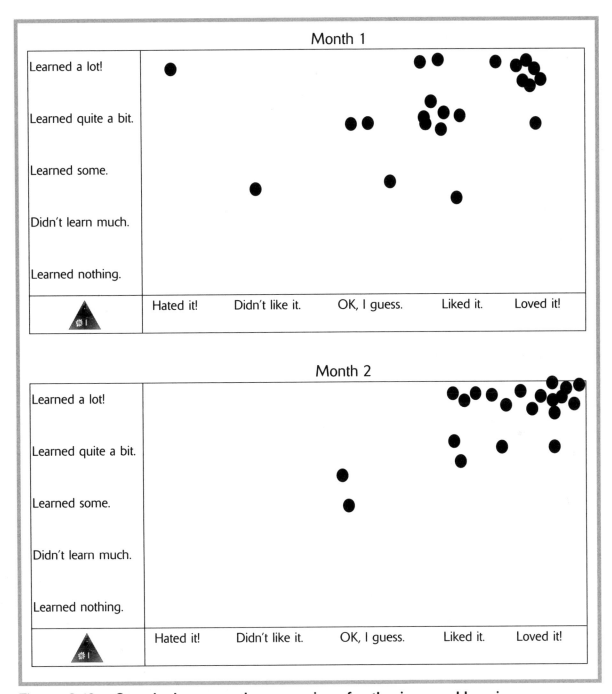

Figure 8.10. Sample three-month progression of enthusiasm and learning.

Month 3					
Learned a lot!					
Learned quite a bit.					
Learned some.					
Didn't learn much.					
Learned nothing.					
	Hated it!	Didn't like it.	OK, I guess.	Liked it.	Loved it!

Figure 8.10. Continued.

though, we slowly reached the point where everyone said that they liked the class and were learning. It suddenly felt as if the students and I were a team working together toward a common goal. The whole feeling in the class changed dramatically in those three months.

I have also found that even though each year is different, the students' wants and needs are generally the same. The improvements that are made through student suggestions one year will also make the next year's students happy and productive. In time, the students start out the first month enjoying and learning, and the teacher's job becomes maintaining enthusiasm and learning.

Key Points

- Student life histories give insight into a child's academic enthusiasm.

- Very often a student's enthusiasm about a subject has nothing to do with the subject itself, but rather *how* it was presented, or *who* presented it.

- The teacher can recapture that lost enthusiasm, because he or she is in charge of these factors.

- History in the making graphs allow a teacher to constantly monitor enthusiasm in the classroom.

- One of the best methods to obtain feedback from the students is the Plus Delta chart.

- Feedback is obtained from the students once a month.

- Student ideas are tallied, discussed, and implemented with the class.

- Ideas that need implementing are tried through the PDSA cycle.

CHAPTER 9

Student Performance and Behavior

Deming's Eighth Point (adapted for the science classroom)

Do not manage the classroom through threats and fear. Work with the students so that they may work most effectively.

Part 1
Improving Performance and Behavior

Performance

When I first began teaching, I set a pattern for reacting in a certain way to particular situations involving student behavior and performance. I would lecture the students and then be frustrated when my exhortation didn't work. When the overall class performance or behavior was out of line, I would give them the standard lecture and hope that things changed. In reality, the students whose behavior needed to change, tuned out after the first two words, and the good students listen patiently, wondering why they have to hear the same lecture again for the hundredth time. That's insanity!

Recently, I realized that if I wanted to improve the students' behavior and performance I had to work *with* the students. The emphasis on continuous improvement set forth by TQM slowly changed my entire perspective. The change in my outlook really struck me one year when the first POW was turned in. In my first-period class there were 28 students. I received 15 POWs. That was just over half the class. I was, to say the least, a bit frustrated. In the next thirty seconds, as I began to fume, I formulated my usual lecture about responsibility and meeting deadlines. I felt the distraught look that always accompanies those lectures developing on my face. As I began to speak, I noticed the faces—the faces that said silently, "Here we go again. Why do I have to listen to this? I turned mine in!" The other faces said, "I don't care now, and I still won't care after you give us a 15-minute lecture." In that instant I knew that the lecture was pointless, and I remembered continuous improvement.

I changed my demeanor and said, "Well, we only got 15 POWs turned in. Could anyone tell me why there weren't more?" The students that had tuned out, turned on. Those lectured to needlessly perked up. The mood in the whole class changed and students began to share ideas. We listed all the reasons that they hadn't turned their work in on time and a lively discussion took place. We used a scientific way of solving the problem. I drew a PDSA chart on the board and asked them to give me ideas on how to help them turn more assignments in on time. They offered some really good suggestions. I'll work throughout the PDSA cycle now to show how it is done.

Plan

In my classroom I had a white board on the wall by the door that showed the assignments that were coming due and those that were late from the previous week. It was designed to help the students remember to turn things in on time. Well, they indicated that it was in a place that they couldn't see very well and never looked. So they suggested that it be moved to the front of the room, where their attention was directed all day. Other students said that they were sometimes confused about the POW question. When they came for help there were too many students hanging out in my room before school, during lunch, and after school for them to get any answers. So they asked if Thursday at lunch could be for POW help only. I said, "Let's try it."

Do

I moved the reminder board to the front of the classroom and instituted a Thursday help day.

Study

The next turn-in day, a few more POWs were turned in. There was improvement, but the amount was still not nearly to my standard.

Act

I kept the same procedure for the next turn-in time, to see if we would improve more.

Study

The next week the turn-in numbers dropped again. I asked students for more suggestions and this time they had none. They actually told me that I was doing all that I could do to help and they were just being lazy. So I told them this: "In this classroom improvement is expected and demanded. The expectations are high here. I'll reach down from these expectations to help you in whatever way I can, but you have to reach up. If you decide not to reach up, its my job to bring you up here anyway, so I'll have to light a fire under you to make you jump up. Now, what kind of fire will make you jump?"

The students pointed out that I shouldn't keep track of the total number of papers turned in each week, but rather the percentage of papers turned in. That way, they said, when the same number were turned in two weeks in a row, there still might be an improvement in the percentage turn in, because people may have been absent. I agreed, and began to track turn-in percentage. I then set the minimum acceptable standard for turn-in rate at 75 percent. If their turn-in percentage improved, regardless of where they were according to the standard, they were okay. But if the turn-in percentage went down and they were not up to the standard, all who didn't turn them in would have lunch detention to do the work. The students and I decided this wasn't a punishment; it just gave those who didn't turn in the assignment time in their busy day to finish it.

There are continuously opportunities to use the PDSA cycle with the students. In another example, my teaching team scheduled a nonacademic day as a reward to those students that had been keeping up on their work and had good grades. The qualifications for going were that they could have no missing assignments *and* have at least a C in each class. When the final deadline for work turn-in came, only 70 out of 140 students qualified. Many students didn't believe that they couldn't go if they had a B yet had a missing assignment. From past experience, students had grown used to having exceptions made for them, but this time we stayed firm on our qualifications. Although we were a little surprised and disappointed that so many had not taken us seriously, we decided to make this a base line, or starting point for improvement. We would shoot for having more students qualify the next time.

Predictably, when the day came, those who did not qualify—and therefore had a slightly altered academic day—were upset. It was a challenging day for the teachers who stayed with the nonqualifying students. At the end of the day, rather than following my first instinct and lecturing the students who stayed back, I decided to use PDSA.

We all sat down—those who qualified and those who didn't—set guidelines for the discussion, and put a transparency of the Plus Delta/PDSA chart on the overhead (Figure 8.8). I told the students that I was disappointed in the attitudes and behaviors that occurred that day. I was curious to find out what they saw and felt. We then brainstormed things that had gone well that day and things that they would have liked to see done differently. Both students that qualified to go and students that did not were in the same room, so there were different perspectives and feelings about both the qualification process and the events of the day. The discussion that transpired was truly remarkable. The students debated the fairness of the qualifications, the interest of the activities that we did, and how the final decisions should be made on whether someone should go. Then we listed the ways in which the teacher and students could make sure that more students would qualify the next time. The part that especially interested me was that the discussion about qualifications was not predictable. Some of the students that didn't qualify still thought that the standard should remain the same or be higher. Some students that did qualify thought the standard should be lower. I was surprised with each person who spoke.

The discussion and the subsequent plan for improvement turned what was a very negative experience for most of the students into a generally positive one. Most students left feeling hopeful and had a clearer idea of how they could qualify the next time. One student who was particularly struck by the whole process came to me at the end of the period and said, "Mr. Burgard, not once in my entire school career has any teacher ever asked me, or the class, how the *teacher* could improve. Thanks."

The key to this type of work with the students is that a standard should be set and improvement toward that standard should be expected. The students can help decide what the standard should be and what the "fire" should be if they do not meet expectation. As a junior high teacher, I've had to light the fire quite a few times, but the students have begun to improve. They improve because suddenly they are actually *part* of the improvement process, not just subject to it.

Demings Fifth Point (adapted for the science classroom)

Constantly improve every activity in the classroom, in order to improve the quality and production of the teacher and each student, while decreasing the likelihood of failure.

Behavior

I never send students to the office unless they threaten harm to other students or myself, or cause enough disruption that the class cannot continue. In my experience, sending students to the office has very rarely, if ever, helped students to improve. The students usually know very well what they need to do to improve, and they know that they have the power to do it.

When students misbehave in my class they are required to do a Plus Delta and PDSA on themselves. They indicate what they do well and what they need to change. Then they are required to formulate improvement ideas for themselves, and plans for these things to occur. Then we implement their plans. The PDSA cycle requires that the plan is done, studied, and acted upon. If their plan works, we continue. If not, they need to come up with another plan.

W. Edwards Deming said that people don't learn through experience, they learn through theory. The PDSA cycle lets students develop a theory for improving their behavior, see if it works, and then learn from the experience. One of my favorite things to say to my students is "Show me, don't tell me." The results in the classroom show both my students and I if their theories work.

Some students are uncomfortable with improvement. One young man was a truly brilliant student, but a bit hyperactive and distracting. He caused a lot of disruptions in class and was continually asked to find ways to improve. He came to the teachers on our team midway through the year and requested to switch teams. When asked why, he said, "Well, on the other team when I misbehave, I just get a detention or sent to the office. I can do that. But here

I always have to change what I'm doing. I always have to improve." Like many of us, he would much rather take redundant ineffective punishment than have to change. He eventually did transfer.

Once the students are used to this PDSA process they come to expect it. They even desire it over a letter grade. Once, about halfway though the year, after the students did their monthly Plus Delta/PDSA evaluating the class, the students asked if I could do a Plus Delta/PDSA for each of them. This, they said, would allow them to see what I saw as their strengths and what I thought they needed to change. This led to a whole discussion on how effective report cards and letter grades are. Junior high students are not stupid. They know that a letter grade does not accurately reflect what they know or how hard they are trying. The *students* wanted to have a more accurate reflection of their performance and how to improve.

Part 2
Evaluating Behavior and Performance with Rubrics

After the students have become familiar with being asked to improve in all areas, the challenge becomes to evaluate those areas in an objective and consistent way so that improvement can be tracked. The most effective method I have found to accomplish this is a modified rubric similar to the ones used when evaluating the POW. Rubrics are adaptable to nearly any situation that needs objective evaluation. Once the students get used to them, they become very good at making them. The following rubrics were designed by students. Each covers a different type of situation and shows how versatile rubrics are.

Evaluating Behavior with Substitute Teachers

When a substitute teacher comes, she is in an awkward position. Most of the time she doesn't know the students or how the class runs. So she has a difficult time evaluating the students' performance accurately. The students, on the other hand, are unsure what criteria the substitute will use to evaluate them. When there are differing standards, it's hard for the regular teacher to get an accurate view of the day's events. I wanted the substitute teacher to be able to effectively evaluate what the class was like, so that I could begin to work with the class to improve.

When I suggested creating a rubric for the substitute teacher to evaluate them, the students were excited to begin. They helped me develop a rubric that helped the sub give an accurate evaluation of their performance, and helped me collect data to make improvements (Figure 9.1).

There is a chart on the Continuous Improvement Board in my classroom that is a performance run chart for how the students perform with substitute teachers. Sometimes, however, a substitute may not use the rubric properly. So, when I come back after a substitute has been there, I'll ask the students to quietly rate their own behavior according to the rubric. The students are usually very honest.

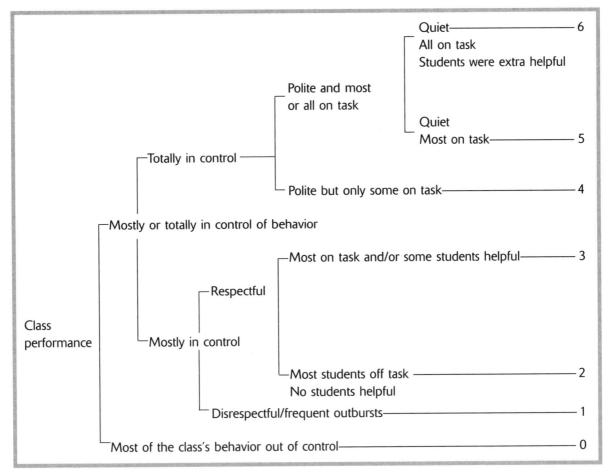

Figure 9.1.   Substitute evaluation rubric.

Once when I came back from a conference, I found that the substitute had given my first-period class a rating of 0. The substitute writes this rating to me on a private note, so the students didn't know. I had the students evaluate themselves before I revealed it. The majority of the students gave the class a 2—not great, but not a 0. In the following discussion, I discovered that the students had in fact finished all of their work, but a little early. Then they talked a lot! The students and I figured that the substitute must have made her decision based upon the last 5 or 10 minutes of class. Also, they are a class that can accomplish a lot in a noisy environment. I'm just used to it. Although it is still not acceptable that they were unruly at the end, the rubric in combination with the discussion cleared up a lot.

The students and I then developed a plan of behavior for the next time a substitute came. The PDSA cycle was brought out once again, and we looked to make improvements. The next substitute report was much better.

When teachers work *with* the students to improve all aspects of their performance and behavior, the students come to know that improvement is not optional. Most students respond because the teacher is working with them to help them become better.

Evaluating Assignment Performance

For a time, the students and I were creating rubrics for every type of assignment that we had. We had project rubrics, lab report rubrics, presentation rubrics, and so on. The students had just about had enough of the rubric game. The history teacher had a bunch of her own rubrics too. The students were just overloaded, and they let us know on their Plus Delta Charts! We heard their cry. Over a few hours on the phone, their history teacher, Shelly Carson (the author of the history book in this series), and I discovered the quality factors in each rubric were nearly identical. So we developed an *assignment rubric* that covered it all! (See Figure 9.2.) Each assignment would have its own criteria, but the quality factors would remain the same.

When I gave the students this final assignment rubric, they literally cheered! Assignments of many types can be charted just like the POW in chapter 6. A blank Assignment progress chart is provided in Figure 9.3.

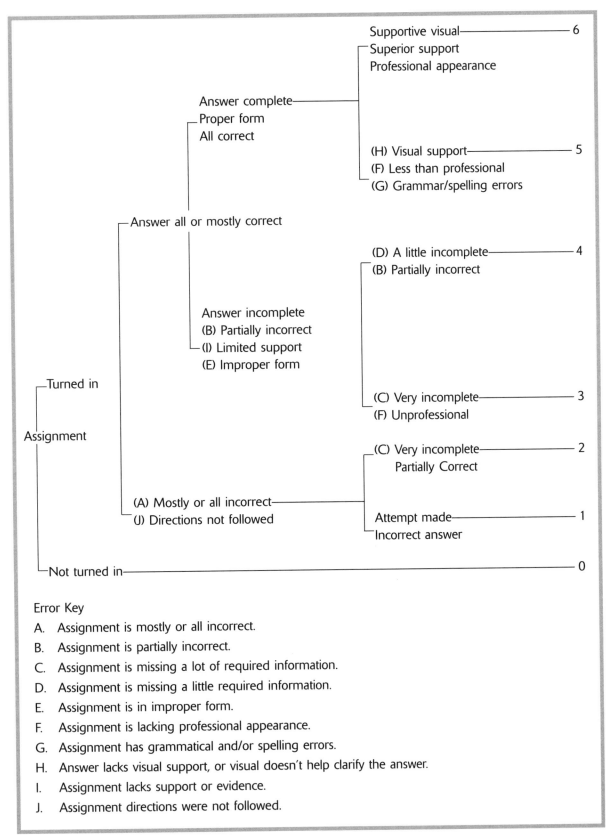

Figure 9.2. Assignment rubric.

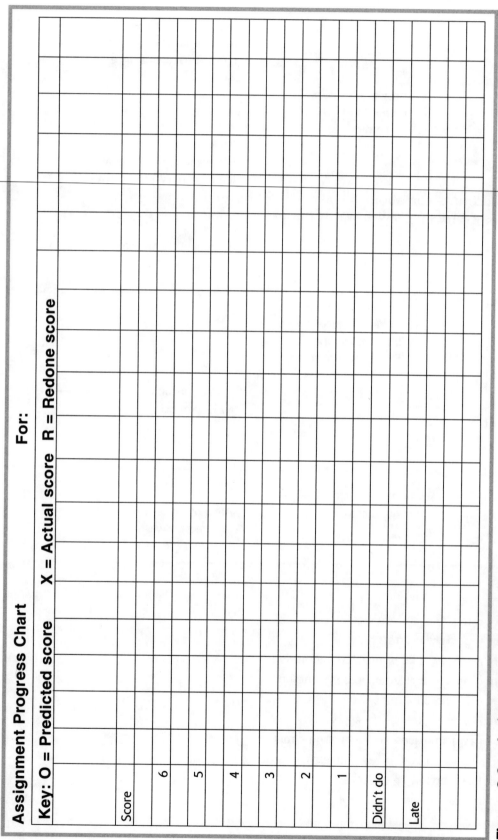

Figure 9.3. Assignment progress chart.

Evaluating Performance with Partners or Groups

In this age of group work in the classroom, it's hard to tell who is really doing the work. Many times one or two students do most of the work, but the whole group shares the grade. The students know that this is unfair and so do I. It came up in one of our Plus Delta discussions as something that needed to change, so I listened.

Now all group work has three grades associated with it. I give each student a role, or a certain function, that he is responsible for. This individual role accounts for about 65 percent of the grade. The group grade, which counts for about 25 percent of the grade, comes from the rubric which was discussed above. The last 10 percent comes from each student's work ethic. The students, once again, helped me to design a 4-point rubric for work ethic. (The number of points that a rubric has is not important. What is important is that it is understood by all and easy to follow.) The work ethic rubric can be found in Figure 9.4.

At the end of each group project, the students evaluate each other and themselves according to the rubric. I then take an average of the scores for the work ethic and add it to the final project grade and the individual role grade. The way it is set up, work ethic can mean the difference of a whole

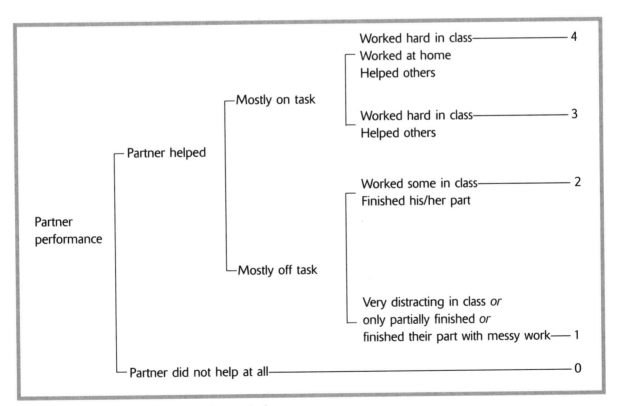

Figure 9.4.   Partner evaluation rubric.

grade level to each student. I have had different students in the same group receive As and Fs.

I no longer hear the students in my class complain that the grading on projects is unfair, primarily because it *is* fair. Thay also have a hard time complaining when they helped design it.

There are countless uses for the rubric. As long as each quality factor is operationally defined so that it is clear to all involved, rubrics are tremendously useful. (Quality factors and operational definitions were discussed in chapter 6.) They can be designed by the teacher, the students, or both. Teachers don't have to track improvement with everything that they use rubrics for. But if there is a desire to see improvement, it is very easy to make a run chart and begin to keep track.

Key Points

- Students can give great insight into how to improve their own performance.

- Students need to be asked what they need in order to improve.

- This puts the students in charge of improvement, and the teacher becomes the provider of the means of improvement.

- Plus Delta charts and PDSA cycle again can be used in the process.

- The attitude this creates in the classroom is that of "we" rather than "teacher-student." Even though each has defined roles—the students provide information into the working of the system and the teacher yields the power to make adjustments—it is a team effort as each performs those roles.

- All types of behaviors and performance can be evaluated and subsequently monitored and improved through the use of rubrics.

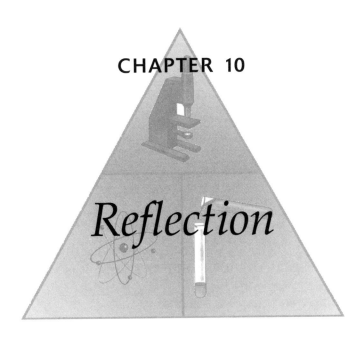

CHAPTER 10

Reflection

Reflection on what has been learned is an important part of the learning process. Yet how often do teachers have students sit back and reflect on the information and knowledge gained over the course of a semester or year? Usually the only reflection that a student gets on his learning is the report card that comes in the mail. But that is not a reflection of the learning that has taken place, but rather a final evaluation of his overall performance. Students need a way to reflect on what they have done and the learning that has occurred. There are many different ways the students can reflect on their learning and experience. The ones I use are *the mind map* and the *self-evaluation form*.

The Mind Map

When teachers plan a unit or a year, they usually put the lessons in a particular order so that they flow and make sense. I call this telling a story. I always hope that the students understand the reasons behind the order that I teach the units, but do the students really see the connections that I have tried to make? How would I be able to tell? A Mind Map is one way of finding out.

In a mind map, the students visually represent areas of study. The picture that they create is a wonderful way to reflect on what they have learned. For

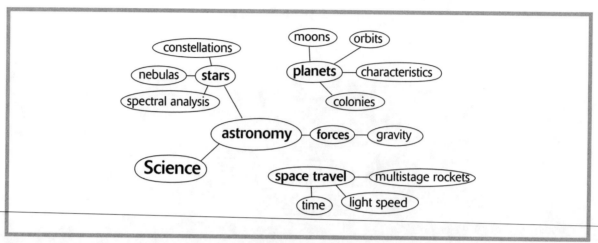

Figure 10.1. Beginning mind map for astronomy.

example, if the area of study is astronomy, the teacher can have the students do a mind map that looks like Figure 10.1 at the end of the astronomy unit.

In the picture, the major topics that were covered in astronomy radiate from the word *astronomy*. Each of the major topics then have the specific things that the students learned radiate from them. I have the students then draw lines from one topic to another. The lines are drawn to show any relationships that exist between the two. This visual representation really brings concepts together for students. (See Figure 10.2.)

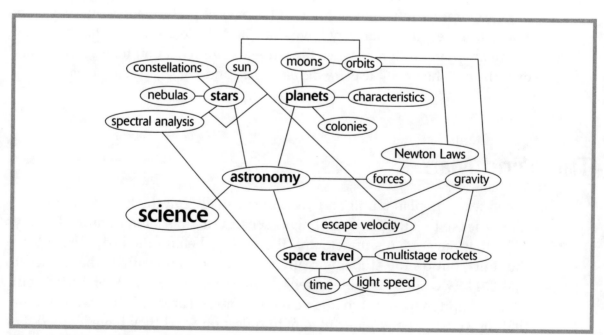

Figure 10.2. Mind map with some connections.

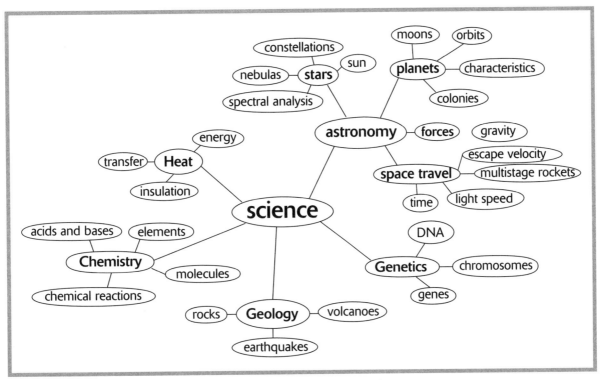

Figure 10.3. Mind map with connections to other topics.

When the students do this at the end of a unit, it not only gives them a chance to reflect and see the connections, but is also an invaluable tool for the teacher to evaluate himself. This is a visual representation of how the students' minds saw the events that took place in the classroom. Does it match what the teacher had hoped for? Does it give new insights that were not planned? It is often very eye opening to the students to be able to visualize patterns and connections that the teacher has made.

The first time through, I do the map with the students to show them how it is done. Usually, after they see and understand what I'm trying to show, the students will begin to suggest connections in addition to the ones that I had planned. As they become more confident and aware, they begin to talk in class about the way that current assignments connect with other assignments they have done.

At the end of each unit, I have them add the newly finished unit to the picture. We are ultimately constructing a visual representation of everything we do throughout the year. When they add additional units to the picture, the students can then make connections from one unit to the next. They begin to see the system that is used to convey information and knowledge to them. Figure 10.3 shows a simple example of a map that can become very complex.

The best way to draw the map is on a large (20 × 30) piece of construction paper or butcher paper. The advantage to butcher paper is that it can be rolled up, carried, and stored easily. The construction paper is obviously stronger. Whichever you choose, make sure that the students have plenty of room to draw and write.

If you are on an interdisciplinary team, this can be incredibly fun and complex. The students can create mind map in each class, making connections within each subject. Then the students can make a big combined map that encompasses their eighth-grade year. Connections are made between curricular areas, not just units. The name of the team then becomes the center point, and the subject names radiate from there. Each subject map from the students' different classes is simply placed around the team name. If the teachers are truly doing interdisciplinary things, the students will have no trouble making the connections. They begin to see their education as a complete system that extends outside each classroom to incorporate all subjects. They see that things in school and life do interconnect and come together.

The simplified map in Figure 10.4 shows some of the ways my teaching team, Team USA, has connected the subject areas. The students see connections that were planned and some that weren't planned at all.

You can see what an incredible visual this is for the students. Whether it can be done with a whole team of teachers or just in the science classroom, the mind map shows clearly the thought process of the students in class.

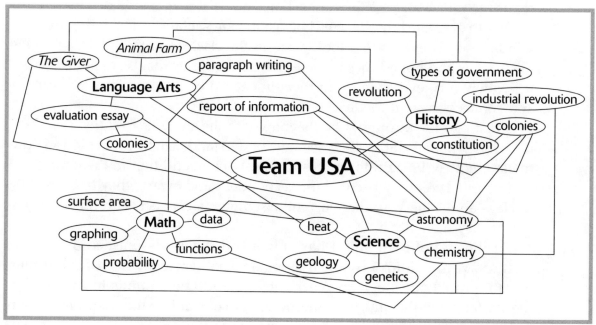

Figure 10.4. Interdisciplinary mind map.

Student's Personal Evaluation

Giving students a clear objective grade has often been a struggle for me. Giving the students a letter grade based strictly on points and percentages didn't seem as though it took into account the many factors that play a role in student performance. The letter grade also didn't seem to give the parents an idea of exactly how the student was doing. A student could be improving her attitude, Weekly Ten scores, and Problem of the Week scores, and it still may not show up on the report card. I decided to have the students use the data that they had been collecting about information, knowledge, enthusiasm, and learning to evaluate themselves and show their parents exactly what their classroom life was like.

The *student personal evaluation form*, shown in Figure 10.5, gives the teacher and the students a tool for looking at each student in a more complete way. It gives parents a wonderful picture of their children, both in their academic progress and their attitude in class. It can also show a lack of improvement, and is therefore an excellent reality check for the students themselves.

Contained on the page is a small version of each student's Weekly Ten run chart, Problem of the Week progress chart, enthusiasm run chart, and error chart. Also included is a space for his/her percentage score in the class. Students enter in their percentage score and then compare it with their improvement data. They take these forms home to copy the data they have been collecting in their continuous improvement journals onto the evaluation form. They are then required to analyze their own progress and performance. On the bottom of the page they write a short letter to the teacher, using the data to explain what grade they should receive and the reasons why. The parents then sign the form, to acknowledge that they have seen it, and send it back.

This doesn't mean that the students determine their grades; it just gives students and parents a great visual representation of the reasons behind the grade. When confronted with the facts of their performance, most students grade themselves appropriately. All see the difference between their percentage and their improvement. One student, when he saw all the data collected on his self-evaluation, said with eyes wide, "This is why I'm getting a D, huh?" Seeing it all in front of him finally made it click.

I simply write a short note back expressing my agreement or disagreement with their reasoning. The teacher can never again be perceived as the bad guy who subjectively hands out grades, because the data tell the story.

This method is very effective on its own, or it can be used in conjunction with the Plus Delta chart in chapter 9. When the Plus Delta chart is used, the students can sit down by themselves or with their parents to reflect on what they have done well and what they need to change, and to develop a plan to accomplish that change.

Name _____

Class percentage _____

Reproduce all the graphs from your life journal on the graphs below. Then, after looking carefully at the graphs,

determine if you agree with the grade the percentage gives you. If, due to *improvement* you believe that your grade

should be higher, justify yourself in the space below. Be sure to refer to the graphs to support your argument.

POW Progress Chart   For:

Key – O = Predicted score			X = Actual score		R = Rewrite score												
POW #	1	2	3	4	5	6	7	8	9	10	11	12	13	14	15	16	17	18	19

Score

6

5

4

3

2

1

Didn't do

Late

Weekly Ten Facts Scores   For:

Place a dot in each square of the score you achieved this week.

Score

10

9

8

7

6

5

4

3

2

1

0

Week | 1 | 2 | 3 | 4 | 5 | 6 | 7 | 8 | 9 | 10 | 11 | 12 | 13 | 14 | 15 | 16 | 17 | 18 | 19 | 20 | 21 | 22 | 23 | 24 | 25 | 26 | 27 | 28 | 29 | 30 | 31 | 32 | 33 | 34 | 35 | 36

POW Error Chart   For:

Shade the box next to each error made.

POW #	1	2	3	4	5	6	7	8	9	10	11	12	13	14	15	16	17	18	19

Possible errors

All or most incorrect (a)

A little incorrect (b)

A lot missing (c)

A little missing (d)

Improper form (e)

Not professional (f)

Grammar and spelling (g)

Visual support problem (h)

Incomplete support (i)

Follow directions (j)

Loved it!

Liked it.

OK, I guess.

Didn't like it.

Hated it!

September   October   November   December   January   February   March   April   May   June

Explain the grade you believe you should receive. (Use the back if neccessary.)

_____

_____

_____

_____

Figure 10.5.   Student personal evaluation.

Key Points

- Students need to reflect on what they have done to see how it all fits together.

- The mind map is a great way of helping students see that things in the curriculum are systemic too.

- The personal evaluation graphs help the student to see all areas of their academic life in one place, so that they fully understand the grades that they receive.

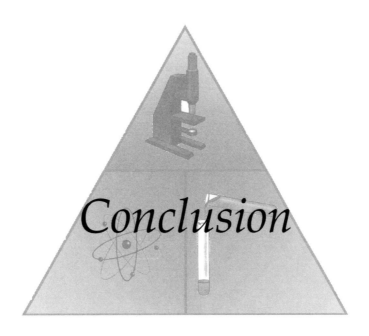

Conclusion

In my eight years of teaching, there has never been a theory or philosophy that enabled me to manage my classroom's learning and behavior in such a positive way. The real validity of the continuous improvement program has been in the students' response, and in the sense of sanity it has given me. No longer is there an adversarial feeling between myself and the students. What was once "me and them" has become "we."

I taught language arts for three years, and I had a motto for their writing— "Practice makes progress." It was a great motto, yet I didn't really have the tools to collect the data to prove my feelings of improvement are real. I stopped using that motto when I switched to teaching science, because I couldn't figure out how to measure improvement in the science classroom. Now, with the tools provided by TQM and the principles put forth in Deming's theory of profound knowledge, I can use that motto once again.

Their training in continuous improvement encourages students to strive for improvement throughout their lives. I know it has had an effect on me. Recently, I had the students doing an activity that just didn't work. My first thought was "These kids are really blowing it." (This statement shows I still have a way to go.) My second thought was, "It's not a people problem, it's a system problem." So, instead of yelling at the students, I observed and looked for ways to improve the activity the next time.

Lost in thought, I was snapped out of it by a student who asked, "What are you doing?"

I said, "Well, I'm not happy with the way this is going, and I'm looking for ways to improve it next time."

He walked away, shaking his head and saying, "Don't you ever think of anything except how to improve?"

No, I guess I don't.

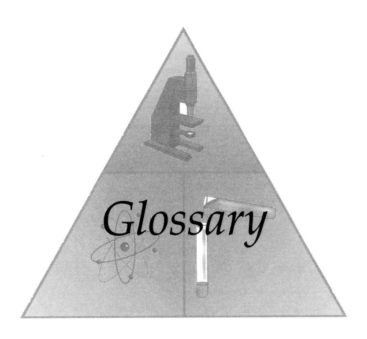

Glossary

Affinity Diagram   a planning tool used to organize ideas into natural groupings in a way that stimulates new, creative ideas

Aim   a concise statement of purpose for the classroom. It is the answer to a student who asks, "Why do we have to be in this class?"

ASQ   a society for advancing individual and organizational performance excellence worldwide by providing opportunities for learning, quality improvement, and knowledge exchange

Class run chart   a graph on the wall on which the teacher tracks the progress of the class as a whole

Common causes of variation   causes that are inherent in any process all the time

Continuous improvement board   same as Improvement Board

Dichotomous key   a way of objectively grading through a series of choices

ELL teacher   teacher of an English Language Learner

Epistemology   the study or theory of the origin, nature, methods, and limits of knowledge

Error chart   a chart used by students to keep track of the types of quality factors that they are not obtaining in papers and projects

Feedback   comments on the success or failure of a particular program from customers

Fishbone Diagram (cause and effect diagram)   a diagram that illustrates causes and subcauses that lead to an effect. It looks like a fish skeleton.

Histogram   a graphic summary of variation in a set of data. It allows the viewer to see patterns that are difficult to see in a table of numbers.

Improvement board   a large board in the classroom containing charts that track the class's progress on tests and in learning and enthusiasm.

Improvement journal   a booklet given to and maintained by each student. It contains all the personal graphs, charts, and information the student needs to track his/her progress.

Information   data transferred into an ordered format that makes it useable and allows one to draw conclusions. In this book, these data are the facts students need to learn during the course of a year.

Knowledge   the ability to use information to create a better future by relating past to current events, solving problems, and utilizing the scientific method

Mentors   those who have been through a given program or experience and help newcomers to the program

Mind map   a visual representation of what has been learned through the year and how it interrelates. It is the first step in creating the Book of Knowledge.

One-hundred-sided die   a special die, containing numbers from one to one hundred, purchased at a school-supply or gaming store

Operational definition   definitions that apply to definite application of words or terms used. Especially when defining Quality Factors essential outstanding work.

PDSA cycle Plan-Do-Study-Act. A four-step process for quality improvement. A different way of looking at the scientific method to solve systemic problems in the classroom.

Plus Delta chart a way to get feedback from students. It is a simple piece of paper with two columns. One side is the Plus side, where students list what they like; the other is the Delta side, where they write the things that need to change.

Problem of the Week (POW) an application or problem-solving question given to the students to evaluate their knowledge

Quality factors a set of criteria that students need to meet in order to produce high-quality papers or projects

Rubric an objective method of grading performance and/or behavior, often on a scale of 1 to 6

Run chart a form of trend analysis that uses a graph to show process measurement on the vertical axis against time. In this book, it is a graph used by students to record test results on which the number correct is the vertical axis and the particular week is the horizontal axis. It is used for both the Weekly Ten scores and Problem of the Week scores.

Scatter diagram a graphical technique for analyzing the relationship between two variables. Used in this book to find the relationships between how the students are feeling about the class and whether they feel as though they are learning.

Scatter matrix representation of all the students' scores on a particular test showing how many students earned each score

Science life history a paper filled out by the students showing how they have felt about science throughout their academic careers

Special cause variation causes of variation that arise out of special circumstances not inherent in the process. In the classroom, this would be an event outside the normal classroom environment that affects the steady improvement of the class, or of the individual student, as indicated by the run charts.

Student run chart a personal graph on which each student tracks her/his progress by recording the number he/she got correct each week

Student self-evaluation form   a reproduction of student-collected data used by the students to evaluate their academic performance and attitude

Supply   the raw materials in the classroom; a teacher's supply consists of all the students in lower grades before they enter his/her classroom

System   a network of connecting processes that work together to accomplish the aim of the system

Total Quality Management (TQM)   a management approach to long-term success through customer satisfaction. It is based upon on the participation of all members of an organization in improving processes.

Variation   a change in data; deviation in form, condition, appearance, or extent from an assumed standard

Weekly Ten   a method of quizzing students every week on a certain number of random facts that they need to know by the end of the year. The number chosen on the quiz is the square root of the total number of facts that they need to know.

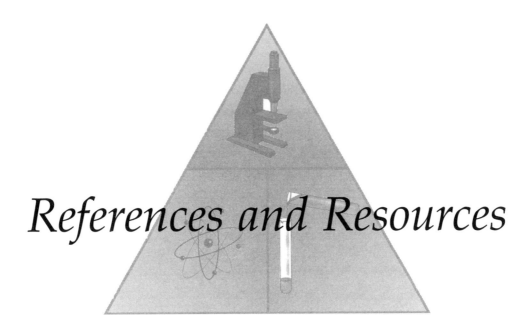

References and Resources

The following is a list of books that I have used as references, and books that I would suggest that you read to further your own quality journey.

References

Deming, W. E. 1992. *The New Economics for Industry, Education and Government*. Cambridge, MA: MIT Center for Advanced Engineering Study.

Deming, W. E. 1986. *Out of the Crisis*. Cambridge, MA: MIT Center for Advanced Engineering Study.

Improvement Tools for Education (K–12). 1992. QIP.

Jenkins, Lee. 1995. *Improving Student Learning*. Milwaukee, WI: ASQC Quality Press.

Recommended Resources

Bernhardt, Victoria. 1998. *Data Analysis for Comprehensive Schoolwide Improvement*. Larchmont, NY: Eye on Education.

Bostingl, John Jay. 1996. *Schools of Quality*. Alexandria, VA: Association for Supervision and Curricular Development.

Byrnes, Margaret. 1994. *Quality Fusion*. Cornesky and Associates.

————. 1997. *Quality Tools for Educators*. Pro Que.

McClanahan, Elaine and Carolyn Wicks. 1993. *Future Force*. Chino Hills, CA: Pact Publishing.

Schargel, Franklin. 1994. *Transforming Education Through Quality Management*. Princeton, NJ: Eye on Education.

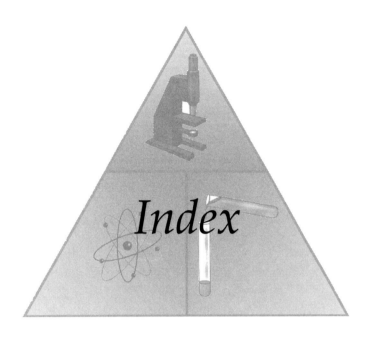

Index